Everyday
Life in Traditional
Japan

The black castle of Matsumoto

C. J. DUNN

Everyday Life in

TRADITIONAL
JAPAN

DRAWINGS BY
LAURENCE BRODERICK

B. T. BATSFORD LTD
LONDON
G. P. PUTNAM'S SONS
NEW YORK

B. T. BATSFORD LTD
4 FITZHARDINGE STREET, PORTMAN SQUARE
LONDON W.I
G. P. PUTNAM'S SONS
200 MADISON AVENUE, NEW YORK NY 10016
TEXT © C. J. DUNN 1969
ILLUSTRATIONS © B. T. BATSFORD 1969
FIRST PUBLISHED 1969
7134 1683 1

PRINTED AND BOUND IN
GREAT BRITAIN BY JARROLD AND SONS LTD
LONDON AND NORWICH

PREFACE

Life in Japan has always had a highly individual flavour. This has not meant that the Japanese have been averse to accepting influences from abroad, and indeed, for most of her history Japan has received many foreign importations—which she has invariably modified to suit her own needs—first mainly from China, and during the last hundred years from the West, more recently especially from America. However, there was one long and important period during which the opposite was true, that of the rule of the Tokugawa Shoguns, and that is the period that is the subject of this book.

A visitor from the West is constantly made aware of what seems to him a duality in Japanese life, a mixture of Western and traditional ingredients. Japan, for all the modernity of its economy and for all the impatience that many young Japanese show towards their country's past, has nevertheless retained very much that is characteristically Japanese. Much of it—and this is true of any country that has a history—comes from the past. The political structure of this past is that which came to end in the middle of the nineteenth century, in dramatic manner, with the Meiji Restoration of 1868. It had been inaugurated in 1603, when Tokugawa Ieyasu took over the supreme power as military dictator; after a settling-down period, civil strife came to an end, and there followed more than two centuries of freedom from large-scale conflicts, and also of almost complete isolation from the outside world. This was a time of great stability, in which what was to be the tradition behind present-day Japan thickened and gelled, so that, although there was in fact a certain amount of development within these centuries, they present a largely consistent appearance.

We can, therefore, consider the period from about 1600 to 1850, the years of undisputed Tokugawa rule, as those of 'Traditional Japan', and the aim of this book is to give the general reader a picture of the background to living in Japan in Tokugawa times.

I wish to express my thanks to my wife, who read and typed the manuscript, and to Mr Peter Kemmis Betty, of Batsford's, for much help during the preparation of this book, and especially for his care in the final selection of the pictorial material. I should also like to thank Mr L. Broderick for his splendid drawings, which have provided many illustrations that could not otherwise have been included. The reader will find other vivid pictures of life in pre-Meiji Japan in the colour prints of contemporary artists such as Hiroshige and Hokusai.   C. J. DUNN

ACKNOWLEDGMENT

The author and publishers would like to thank the following for the illustrations appearing in this book: Hyogensha Co. Ltd, Kyoto for fig. 7; Japanese Ministry of Information for figs. 3, 4, 5 and 6; *Edo Shōbai Zue* by I. Mitani (Seia-bō, Tokyo, 1963) for figs. 10, 45, 46, 47, 48, 51, 53, 54, 56, 57, 59, 61, 65, 66, 68, 72, 73, 75, 76, 77, 81, 82, 83, 84, 85, 88, 90, 91, 93, 94 and 96; and the Victoria and Albert Museum for figs. 52, 79 and 80

CONTENTS

LIST OF

ILLUSTRATIONS

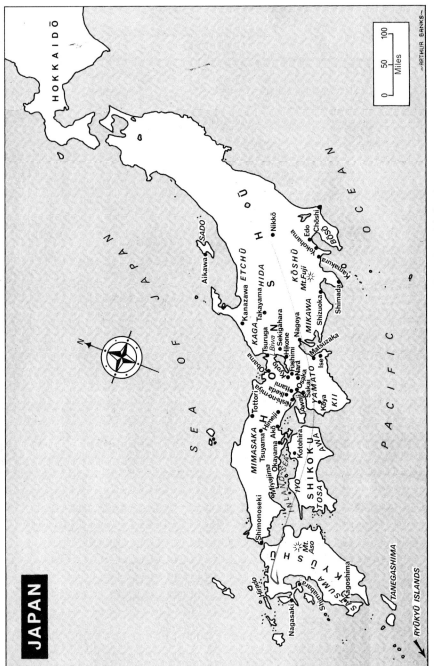

2 Map of Japan, showing places mentioned in this book

I

A country in isolation

The Land
Being at the eastern end of the Asian continental mass, Japan has
a climate in many ways like that of the Northern Atlantic states
of the USA—that is to say, winters are cold (with winds blowing
from Siberia), and summers are hot (with winds from the Pacific).
The cold winds of winter cross the Japan Sea before reaching the
mountainous continent-facing coast of Japan, and as they do so
they pick up moisture; much of this is deposited as snowfall, which
is consistently heavy, often coming up to the eaves of the houses (*3*).
The Pacific side of Japan tends to have bright but cold weather in
winter. In summer, the continent-facing side has clear weather,
while there is cloud on the Pacific coast, so that, particularly in
the south and east, summers are hot and humid. The Japanese
find the heat of their summers more unpleasant than the winter
cold, and build their houses accordingly.

Japan consists of four main islands, with innumerable smaller
ones. The northernmost is Hokkaidō, which was not sufficiently
populated during our period to be of importance. To the south is
Honshū, the main island, somewhat larger than Great Britain,
with Kyūshū and Shikoku lying further south still (*2*). An additional complication to the climatic picture is that, except in
Hokkaidō, there is in June a short but often torrential rainy season,
the northern edge of the monsoons, while another is that from late
July to mid September, Japan, especially its southern regions, lies
in the path of typhoons coming up from the Pacific, so that any
area is liable to be visited by great winds, heavy rainfall, or tidal
waves. As if these possibilities of calamity were not enough, Japan
lies in the earthquake and volcano belt which runs all round the
Pacific basin, and although active volcanoes (*4*) are usually distant

3 Snow scene. This photograph has some television aerials and electric wires, but otherwise gives a good impression of a traditional Japanese scene after a moderate snowfall

from areas of population and damage from eruptions has not been great, earthquakes are part of everyday life, with small shocks constantly reminding the Japanese that disaster could occur at any moment.

On the favourable side of her geographical position, Japan has a low latitude, with the sun higher in the sky and with less variation in length of day than in northern Europe. Winter is short, and so the growing season is long. Warmth and moisture together with fertile alluvial soils in most of the agricultural districts help to make Japan rich in food-crops (5). Japan is very mountainous, but on the hills trees grow abundantly (6), which meant that in our period building was of wood; houses were made of cedar and other durable timber, needing no paint, but very inflammable, so that fires might easily sweep away whole villages or sections of towns if the wind were right. When an earthquake came, however, the frame-houses were pliable and less likely to collapse than if they had been more solidly built of brick or stone.

The People

In common with most of the other inhabitants of the Asian Pacific littoral, the modern Japanese are classified as Mongols, but there seem to be several strains in the population. It is most probable that there has been a mixture of people coming from Korea and North China, from South China, and from the islands of the Pacific, through the Ryūkyū Islands. There are indications that some elements of Japanese culture are derived from the south; domestic architecture, for example, may have some connection with that of Polynesia.

4 The crater of Mt Aso. This volcano, in Kyūshū, is still active

The Japanese language, even though it has certain similarities of structure with some continental Asian languages like Korean and Mongolian, cannot be shown to have a common descent with them, and the only clearly related language is that of the Ryūkyūs. The sole extraneous ethnic group is formed by the Ainus, now restricted to the island of Hokkaidō in the north; they had all gone from the mainland of Japan long before the seventeenth century, and certain place-names, including that of Mt Fuji, are the only relics of their earlier, far wider, occupation, before they were driven out by their successors, the people who, free from invasion themselves,

5 Flooded rice-fields, with terracing on the left. The wide, straight roads are, of course, modern

3

6 Forest of *sugi*, a large tree, like the cedar, near Kyoto, the old capital

forged a strong and homogeneous culture, going back some 2,000 years.

The native Japanese religion, now called *shintō*, 'the way of the gods', has some elements that may derive from the shamanism of northern Asia, but it also includes simple animistic cults, in which trees and rocks, sometimes whole mountains or islands, are worshipped (7). It had as its culmination a set of creation-legends which include an account of the divine origins of the Imperial family.

One important sector of *shintō* is concerned with food-production and fertility, rice-wine and jollity. *Shintō* is also very preoccupied with cleanliness and the avoidance of defilement, and prefers not to have anything to do with death. On the other hand Buddhism, which came to Japan from China through Korea some 1,500 years

7 Miyajima, with its outer gate (*torii*) set in the sea. The whole island, of which some is visible on the left, used to be worshipped as a god, and women and agriculturalists were not allowed on it

4

ago, brought with it, along with glamorous elements of Chinese civilisation and artistic achievement, a new introspection and withdrawal from the world, a concern with the afterlife and an acceptance of death (*8*).

For many centuries these two religions had been complementary: the gods of *shintō* were incorporated into the Buddhist system, even though the two priesthoods and the centres of worship, Buddhist temples and *shintō* shrines, usually retained their independence. Between them the two religions provided, and to a large extent still provide, a background for almost all human activity in Japan, but only a background, not a morality. Morality, the rules of conduct within society, was defined in secular principles, largely derived from Confucianism. These principles included a system of loyalties, in which one's lord came before one's family, and parents before spouse and children, together with an unquestioning acceptance of authority. Sobriety and frugality were required of superior men, while extravagance, whether in dress, emotion or expenditure, was to be deplored, although no more than could be expected from the lower classes, especially from those whose aim was the amassing of money, rather than service to one's lord or one's country. Although the money motive is less reprehensible today, these attitudes are still to be found among the Japanese, and are demonstrated in loyalty to their employers and to their country.

The End of Civil War
Since the twelfth century, when the old rule by the emperor or his courtiers had been replaced by that of military overlords, there had been periodical civil wars in Japan, either between opposing clans or factions, or sometimes involving an emperor trying to regain the authority

8 Stone Buddha, one of a group of unusually large rock-carved Buddhas near Usuki in Kyūshū

5

which his ancestors had enjoyed. These wars had hindered the development of trade, had been an ever recurring danger to crops, and had depleted the country's manpower. It is true that a certain amount of literature had been produced, but it was concentrated in the Imperial and military courts and great religious centres. *Nō* plays, the tea-ceremony and its equipment, the reformation of poetry that led to the 17-syllable *haiku*, all owe their development to this period, but all were restricted to small aristocratic and religious circles.

By the middle of the sixteenth century, however, even though fighting was to continue on and off for another 50 years, conditions began to settle down, and the advancement of commerce and the arts became possible. In 1573, rule over virtually the whole of Japan came into the hands of one man, Oda Nobunaga. He was a passionate and ruthless man; for example, he burnt a whole monastery complex of temples, with all its inhabitants, as part of his plan to take power away from the Buddhist warrior-priests who had been so great a destructive force in preceding years. At the same time he was devoted to the arts, and when he was killed in 1582 by one of his generals (whom he had slighted), the attack on the temple where he was staying occurred while he was dancing a piece from a *nō* play. His successor, Toyotomi Hideyoshi, who continued the work of unifying Japan, is almost as famous for the splendour of his cherry-blossom viewing parties as for his good government of the country and his unsuccessful invasion of Korea.

The wars had dispersed many of the adherents of the Imperial court, so that there were far fewer who resided in the capital, now called Kyoto, and the great annual festivals which had been carried on by these courtiers came to a halt. They were restarted by the townsfolk, and a wave of enthusiasm for participation in this sort of gay ceremonial spread through the cities—the Gion festival, which still trundles its great wagons through the Kyoto streets in July, is an instance of this (9). Other new entertainments were developed: the *fūryū* dances were among these and spread far and wide. They were great jollifications, often connected with the Buddhist *bon* festival in the height of the summer, when the spirits of the dead come back to earth and are entertained with singing and dancing. In the *fūryū*, disguises and fancy dress were assumed, and there was dancing in the streets. Women's fashions became much simpler in form so that movement was easier, but the

6

9 Gion Festival. The wagons, with the shoulder-borne floats that alternate with them, date from the Tokugawa period, though the Festival is much older, having been started in the tenth century in an attempt to terminate an epidemic. Each vehicle belongs to a ward of the city, whose men don traditional dress for the occasion. Those on the roof are there to fend off overhead wires

materials were more elegant in pattern, especially for the wives of merchants.

It was a time when a lively trade was being carried on with the outside world. In 1543 the first Europeans, some Portuguese, had landed in Tanegashima, an island to the south of Kyūshū, and Francis Xavier came in 1549 to start the Jesuit mission. This was so successful that soon the Jesuits had virtual control of the city of Nagasaki, and churches were established even in Kyoto and Osaka. Christian emblems became popular as decorative motifs, and among the disguises worn in the *furyū*, foreign garb, and foreign headgear in particular, had considerable vogue. Strange beasts were exhibited in menageries, and in Kyoto and elsewhere side-shows and puppet-shows were given, as well as crude dramatic performances. Farmers were doubtless less happy than the rest, but the spread of settled government, and a spirit of national unity, partly aroused by the contact with foreigners and in reaction to

7

the threat against national security which their presence seemed to offer, led to an improvement in public morale. The painted screens that were a feature of the period very often illustrate the life of the times, mainly in the towns, with frequent scenes of much activity and jollity.

These entertainments and festivities carried on into the seventeenth century, and became the ancestors of, among other things, the live popular drama. But the spirit of the nation changed, as the puritanical and coldly calculating rule of the Tokugawa family tightened its grip on the country after the death of Hideyoshi in 1598, and the defeat of his son in 1615. Foreign influences dwindled, and prohibitions and persecutions, started under Hideyoshi, became increasingly the lot of Christians in Japan. A largely Christian revolt at Shimabara, near Nagasaki, was put down in 1637, and everything was done to stamp out Christianity, more for political than for religious reasons. At the same time, a policy of seclusion was instituted, the aim of which was to avoid any foreign involvement which might lead to disturbance of internal peace. All Japanese overseas, whether engaged in trade in the South-East Asian peninsula, or as wives or entertainers in Java, were cut off from the homeland, and the only contact with the outside world was through the small and closely supervised Dutch and Chinese trading-stations in Nagasaki, all other foreigners having been expelled. This policy of isolation was reinforced by a prohibition on the building of ocean-going ships, and no Japanese was allowed to leave Japan.

This state of affairs lasted until 1853, when Commodore Perry's ships appeared in Edo Bay, and forced the government to open some ports. Foreigners began to reappear in Japan. The Tokugawa régime, already under internal pressure, with the country seething with great restlessness, lasted only another 15 years before rule passed back to the young Emperor and his supporters: new ideas flooded in, bringing an end to the feudalism of traditional Japan.

The Government after 1603

A description of everyday life in traditional Japan would be difficult if not impossible to understand without some knowledge of how the government of the country was organised, and for this it is necessary to understand the position of the Tokugawas. The founder of their power, Tokugawa Ieyasu, a man of outstanding ability, if not genius, had been an associate of both Nobunaga and Hideyoshi, his predecessors. Under Hideyoshi, he had held the east of Japan, having a fortress at Edo (the present-day capital, Tokyo). When he formally became Shogun in 1603, it was to Edo that he transferred the seat of his government, partly so that it should be surrounded by his supporters and partly because, like some military rulers of earlier times, he considered that the atmosphere of the capital, Kyoto, with its devotion to the fine arts and its sophisticated living, would corrupt the simple virtues of his followers.

After the death of Hideyoshi's son in his stronghold of Osaka Castle, taken in 1615, the greatest immediate threat to Ieyasu's power was removed. He died the next year, but members of the Tokugawa family succeeded one after another in the position of Shogun (which in effect became a hereditary one), having full control of all the land of Japan. Whatever threats there remained to this control, whether from the Emperor, religious groups or military lords, were met with cunning and ruthless efficiency, the government being above all determined to keep the country at peace.

The Emperor in his court at Kyoto was theoretically the source of power, and indeed it was he who gave the Shogun his title. This ancient title, an abbreviation of a longer expression with the meaning of 'Commander-in-Chief for quelling the barbarians', was in effect equivalent to military dictator of the country. Once the Tokugawas had taken over the reins of government, the Emperor's duties were confined to bestowing this title and to conferring lesser titles on such persons as the Shogun nominated. His time was to be spent in literary and ceremonial pursuits; his needs, and those of his courtiers, were met by a grant of land to provide them with an income. His activities were supervised by the Kyoto Deputy, a government official, so that he was a mere figurehead, albeit one widely respected throughout the country. At no time did there cease to be an emperor, lip-service continued to be accorded him, and it was round his person that final revolt against the Tokugawa régime was centred.

Another potential source of opposition was to be found in the Buddhist temples and *shintō* shrines; some of the former had played a considerable role in earlier civil wars. The Shogun kept them under control by a number of Superintendents of Temples and

Shrines, and their incomes were allotted to them from central or local sources which could be cut off if necessary. One Buddhist sect—the Shin sect—of which the Shogun was particularly suspicious was dealt with by a characteristic piece of Tokugawa 'divide and rule' tactics; in the preceding era members of this sect had caused trouble for the military authorities by setting up autonomous communities of commoners, and to prevent this happening again Ieyasu ordered the sect to be split into two branches so that it would have to support separate groups of temples, kept apart and weakened by rival jealousies.

However, such threats as these were very minor compared with that from the hostile military lords. The Tokugawa ruler allotted territories in exchange for an oath of allegiance, and made sure that faithful followers and relatives, including those who had fought with him at Sekigahara in 1600, were given lands in strategic positions—forming a ring of buffer estates round Edo, a string of others protecting the great routes of Japan or keeping watch on possible lines along which potentially hostile lords might advance on Edo. These latter would be from the 'outside' lords, who had surrendered to him at Sekigahara or afterwards. The majority of these were great landowners, and were, in fact, far more wealthy than the Tokugawa adherents. However, the Shogun himself held great estates, and also administered the main cities of Edo, Kyoto and Osaka.

Thus the political control of the country worked through the officials of the directly held lands and through the vassaldom of the lords, who lived under threat of dispossession or transfer as punishment for disloyalty or misconduct. There were controls on the amount of fortification permitted; lords were encouraged to spy on their neighbours and report on suspicious activities, while social contact was frowned on. Then in addition there were government inspectors, whose function was to keep a watchful eye on the lords and make sure that they conducted their affairs in a manner to be approved.

Yet another weapon in the Shogun's armoury for controlling the top strata of society was the compulsory attendance at his court in Edo. In the early days of Tokugawa rule its possible opponents had to leave hostages in Edo as surety for their good behaviour, but later a unified system was evolved. This required alternate residence of one year in Edo and one on his home territory for every large landowner (except for those whose lands were either near by or most distant from the centre of government), involving an annual journey one way or the other. Appropriate residences had to be maintained in Edo, where the wives and families of the lords had to stay. This measure, along with the providing of garrisons for the Tokugawa castles and enforced assistance with certain public works, assured both political and economic control of the wealthy overlords, since the constant travel to and fro, coupled with the maintaining of two establishments in the style that was obligatory for a great lord, involved considerable outlay of income, time and effort.

The rest of the population in town and country was controlled in two ways. First, there were officials appointed by local authorities or by the central government, and these worked through officers who could be termed 'policemen'. The other method was through a system of responsibilities, so that an ordinary Japanese could rarely contravene the accepted code of behaviour without involving others in punishment for his offence: the head of a family answered for its members, groups of households for each individual household, the headman for his village, and any group might be punished for the misdeeds of one of its members.

There was no semblance of a constitution. As regards criminal justice, magistrates had a code to guide them, but this was never published as a whole, although notices about certain crimes were posted from time to time. In principle, there was no punishment without confession, and this often led to a suspect being rigorously interrogated. This criminal code, such as it was, could be changed without warning. This was in keeping with the fundamental Tokugawa attitude, derived from Confucianist precepts, that the people should not be instructed as to what the law might be, but should be content to do what they were told.

These then were the ways in which the Tokugawa Shoguns sought to perpetuate their family's power over every inch of the country, and dominance over every aspect of Japanese life, indeed, over every living soul. Their efforts met with remarkable success for 200 years, although a gradual decline in Tokugawa power set in after the mid eighteenth century. The very nature of Japanese society was in their favour, for the existing class system was a weapon in their hands that required only to be maintained and reinforced in its application. It was only a fairly small number of

Japanese who were unaffected by this rigid division into classes: on the one hand were the courtiers and priests, doctors and some intellectuals, and on the other the outcasts, a motley crew performing a variety of lowly tasks. Everyone apart from these exceptions was either a warrior, a farmer, a craftsman or a merchant.

In this tight class system there was an equally rigid hierarchy, with the warrior class (*samurai*) at the top; the *samurai* enjoyed privileges, such as the right to wear two swords, but also had obligations and were expected to lead sober lives and set a good example to the rest. Next came the farmers (the bulk of the population), placed in this position because on them depended the livelihood, in the form of rice, of the warrior class. The honour was dubious, for severe restrictions were put on their liberty, lest they should leave their farms; their lot was usually a miserable one, compounded of hard work and poverty for most of them. Craftsmen came next, and merchants or traders last. Merchants were despised because it was considered that they produced nothing and were activated solely by the desire to amass wealth; indeed, this they proceeded to do, and the culture of the latter part of the period was mainly their creation, and the growth of their power a leading factor in the decline of the old class system.

Because these classes were so clearly divided, and had quite different ways of living, it will be best to treat them separately, describing the conditions and daily life of each in turn.

2

The Samurai

The population of Japan is estimated at having been slightly under 30 millions for most of the Tokugawa period, remaining remarkably static for this length of time. There were probably fewer than two million who were *samurai*, the highest of the four classes into which the people of Japan were divided. The word *samurai* implies 'servant' and is strictly applicable only to retainers, but the custom arose of applying it to the whole warrior class, who were in any case all liegemen, direct or indirect, of the Shogun himself, the apex of the pyramid.

Membership of the class was hereditary, and included many whose ancestors in earlier times had been farmers, ready to take up arms to fight in local armies. Others had belonged to clans with great estates in the regions distant from the capital, themselves descendants or supplanters of still earlier land-holders under the Emperor when he really ruled Japan. Some *samurai* families had originally been closely connected with the Emperor, who, embarrassed by the financial burden of too numerous descendants, had reduced several groups of his dependants to the rank of ordinary noble in the tenth century, giving them land and so freeing himself from further responsibility. One of these groups had been the Minamoto clan, which increased its land-holdings by predatory means, and which rose to become rulers of Japan in the thirteenth century: the Tokugawa family, which had long held a small domain in Mikawa province, east of Nagoya, before moving to Edo, itself claimed descent from these earlier Shoguns.

During the early sixteenth century there had been considerable mobility between the classes, especially between farmers and warriors, but Hideyoshi endeavoured to stabilise society, and decreed in 1586 that *samurai* could not become townsmen, and that

10 (a) *Samurai* in street. A *samurai*, wearing his two swords, walks by a seaweed shop, followed by an attendant, who carries a package wrapped in the traditional silk cloth (*furoshiki*). The men on the left are slicing up dried seaweed, which was eaten with rice. Over the shop is its *noren* (see p. 115) with the shop sign (repeated on the drawers at the back and on the boxes in the street), and the name of the shop, Nakajima-ya. The chief clerk is writing up the ledger

a farmer could not leave his land. The rigidity of the class system so characteristic of the ensuing centuries really dates from this time, and in the next year farmers had to give up their weapons, in an operation known as 'Hideyoshi's sword-hunt'; henceforward *samurai* alone had the right to carry a sword. A sword in this context is a long sword; a shorter sword was also worn, and the first recognition point for distinguishing a *samurai*, either in illustrations, or probably even at the time in the flesh, is the sight of two sword-handles protruding from the girdle on the left-hand side, where the right hand could come across and draw either (*10*). Townsfolk were allowed to carry a short sword for protection. Farmers had to content themselves with their agricultural implements, as peasants have always had to the world over. Occasionally individuals or groups of non-*samurai* performed a special service and were granted the privilege of wearing 'the large and the small' as the swords were called.

14

鳥屋

(b) *Samurai* at the poulterer's. A *samurai* is leaving the shop, and is replacing in his girdle his large sword, removed to allow him to sit comfortably while conducting his business with the shopkeeper, who is obsequiously seeing him off the premises. Outside the shop, the *samurai's* servant, his *kimono* tucked into the back of his girdle, waits patiently for his master

The warrior class included everyone with the right to wear two swords from the Shogun down, through the great lords in their domains and senior officials in Edo, to minor officials and foot-soldiers. They all received incomes according to their station, and the machinery for distributing these incomes was a fundamental part of the organisation of society. Income was calculated not in money but in rice. The two main groups involved were the warriors themselves, as recipients, and the farmers, as suppliers.

Land was measured not so much by area, as by the estimate of the amount of rice it would produce in a year. The unit of rice used for this purpose was the *koku*, which is equivalent to about five bushels, and would, in fact, feed one person for a year; at the beginning of the seventeenth century surveys indicated that the annual national production was about 25 million *koku*. This was distributed by the Shogun, after keeping about one-fifth of it for his own use, among the lords of the domains—that is to say, land producing this amount was allocated either to the directly held territories, or to the lords, a small amount being granted to the Emperor. The highest allocation was to the 'outside' lords of Kaga, who had their castle in Kanazawa near the north coast: they received 1,300,000 *koku*. Shimazu, of Satsuma (in Kyūshū), had 730,000, and altogether there were, at the beginning of the period, some 270 lords with 10,000 *koku* or over. These lords were the *daimyō*, the great land-holders; and just as the Shogun kept some for himself and distributed the rest, so did the *daimyō*, keeping some of his income for himself and his family and allotting the rest to his vassals in sub-fiefs. The superior vassals had areas of land placed under their control; inferior ones received a stipend measured in *koku*, without land. Lower-ranking persons received rice or rice-equivalent incomes.

Incomes expressed in *koku* referred to the productivity of the land, and the lord had to see to it that he obtained the rice from the farmers, or, to be more precise, that his officials got it from the village headman, who got it from the farmer. The farmer was allowed to keep a proportion of the crop, sometimes six-tenths, but often less; in practice, the recipient took what he was entitled to, leaving the farmer the rest, which would depend upon his harvest. Sometimes the lord, especially if he had only a small allocation, ran out of resources before the harvest was in, and had to squeeze his farmers to pay early, leaving them to make what shifts they could to meet his demands.

It has to be realised that incomes were not normally linked to the job that the recipient was doing, except in the sense that the income fitted a man for his position rather than the other way round. To serve as an official to a lord was part of feudal obligation, and a vassal should not expect to be paid especially for something that it was his duty to do. In the eighteenth century there was a slight modification to this, which allowed the Shogun to give a temporary allowance to a person whose rate of income did not in fact qualify him for a certain position, but whose ability fitted him for it.

The sort of residence that a *samurai* occupied depended upon his status as measured by his income. The Shogun had his castle in Edo (where the Emperor now resides), and most *daimyō* also had a castle (*1*), round which grew a town. Castles came into being in Japan much as they did in Europe, as strongholds for barons fearing attack from their neighbours. The majority still in existence in Japan date from the sixteenth century, for there was little building under the Tokugawas except in Edo, since fortification was strictly controlled, the Shogun being anxious above all that no lord should become strong enough to challenge his power. Until the sixteenth century warriors had tended to live on their farms, and only go to the castle when summoned, but when the warrior and farmer

11 Moat of Osaka Castle. This view clearly shows the profile of the outer wall. The castle was built by Hideyoshi

classes were separated, the former went to live in the towns that had begun to form round the castles to accommodate the people concerned with its supply of goods and services. When the *samurai* moved in, the *jōkamachi*, 'under-castle towns' increased in size and importance, becoming the most usual form of urban development in Japan. All activities in such towns were directed towards the castle and were controlled by it, and the atmosphere in it was quite different from that in Kyoto, where the Imperial court was dominant, and even more so from that of Osaka, a fundamentally mercantile town, in which, it is true, Hideyoshi had built a castle, later the headquarters of the Shogun's Deputy, but which nevertheless managed to retain considerable independence.

The castle usually included the town in its outer defences of ditches. In Edo, for example, existing water-courses were adapted to form a series of more or less rectangular shapes, the innermost containing the castle, the intermediate ones having officials' residences, and the outermost stretching down to the Bay and having merchants and craftsmen living within them. The purpose of the outer ditches was not much more than to slow down an attacker

12 Himeji Castle, known as the 'White Heron', is a great complex of walls and buildings, and illustrates the defensive features mentioned in the text

by making him use existing bridges and thus hamper his freedom of movement.

The castle itself was normally raised on a mound, artificial or otherwise, which was revetted with stonework, the individual pieces being often of very large size and set deep into the soil. These revetments have a characteristic curved contour, a combination of slope at the bottom to maintain stability and near-verticality at the top to deter attackers from climbing up (*11*). Many castles took advantage of natural features to acquire elevation, and an extreme case of this is Gifu, which occupies a steep hill some hundreds of feet above its town, the only access in the past being a steep road up the precipitous face.

The revetments were topped by walls of plastered timberwork, with tiled roofs. Access through gateways was always arranged to have attackers under fire as they approached. There was a keep, with several floors, once again of timber construction with thick plaster-filling and heavily barred windows (*12*). There were slits and embrasures for arrow- and musket-fire, and often downward-facing slits under windows through which missiles could be dropped on attackers. The keep was crowned with graceful tiled

13 Audience chamber in Nijō Castle, with wax figures of the Shogun and his lords, in court dress. To the Shogun's left is his sword-bearer, behind whom is the room in which lurked the bodyguard

roofs, often with gilded ornaments. The living quarters were not in the keep, but in separate dwellings within the castle complex.

When the castles were built, they were expected to have to withstand swords and spears, arrows and battering-rams and the use of fire, but certainly no heavy artillery. The firearms brought in by the Portuguese and others were limited to muskets, pistols and some small cannon. A certain amount of iron reinforcement to gates, and rounded embrasures for muskets (as distinct from the slits required by archers), were all the modifications that were needed. The Shogun naturally did his best to ensure that no advanced weapons got into the hands of his potential foes. Moreover, from being a stronghold against neighbouring lords, these castles became rather a defence against possible attack by rebellious townsmen or revolting peasants, who were not likely to be well disciplined or to be equipped with other than simple weapons. Thus not much more was required than stout gates and steep approaches.

One of the most magnificent of these castles is that built by Ieyasu at Kyoto in the first decade of the seventeenth century. More of a palace than a castle, it was used as the Shogun's lodging when he came to Kyoto; it was in a grandiose style, partly to rival the Emperor's palace, and partly to compete with the glories of Hideyoshi's castle (which Ieyasu later had destroyed) outside Kyoto. Nijō Castle is still surrounded by a wall and moat, and the mound on which the keep was built remains, although the keep itself is gone. The palace is basically a series of rooms, the floors covered by *tatami*—thick straw mats finished with woven grass, the standard flooring in houses of the well-to-do. The rooms are divided from the corridors which run outside them by sliding screens, while the corridors are separated from the outside world by screens of wooden lattice covered with paper to let in light, with further heavy wooden screens, like shutters, that would be moved over at night and in bad weather. The rooms nearest the entrance were for visiting lords, and the more worthy of trust a person was, the nearer he could approach the audience chamber (*13*) and the private apartments. Near the Shogun's position in the audience chamber were some compartments which concealed soldiers posted there ready to dash out in an emergency, while the silent approach of a would-be assassin could be detected because of the special construction of the plank floor of the 'nightingale' corridor which makes it 'sing' as one walks along it.

The *koku*-rating of *samurai* was used in all sorts of circumstances. Below *daimyō* with their minimum of 10,000 *koku*, it determined the area of the plot on which a *samurai* was allowed to build. For example, 8,000 *koku* entitled him to about two acres, 2,000 *koku* to about one acre, while the lowest income of five bales of rice gave the right to about 280 square yards. In fact, the lowest grades lived more or less communally, in 'long houses', divided into apartments with some degree of shared accommodation. A typical arrangement was to have a gateway with a row of rooms as its upper storey. Lastly, there were some *samurai* who had no official income at all and no right to a residence; these were the masterless men, the *rōnin*, who had either abandoned their allegiance or whose master had been deprived of his post. The *rōnin* were some of the freest inhabitants of traditional Japan, since they maintained their *samurai* status without the burden of its duties, but forgoing its assured sustenance. They earned a living as best they could: some became writers, Confucian scholars or school-teachers; some, instructors in swordsmanship or other military arts; others traded on their ability with their weapons and hired themselves out as

14 (a) *Samurai* in *naga-bakama*.　　　　(b) *Samurai* in *kami-shimo*

bodyguards and trouble-shooters for rich merchants. While they were earning, they could afford comfortable accommodation; when things went less well, they had to live at best in temples, at worst in what rough shelter they could find.

Rank was also reflected in clothes. For ceremonial occasions and when on duty, the *samurai* wore clothes as shown in figure *14b*. The formal part of his attire is the *kami-shimo*, the combination of 'upper and lower', that is, an over-jacket (*kataginu*) with stiffened shoulders and trousers (*hakama*), more like a divided skirt; the trousers had a very low crotch, and openings at the sides, and were held in place by two sets of ties on the front and rear parts, fastening round the waist. On ordinary occasions for *samurai* of all ranks, and for lower-ranking ones at all times, these trousers finished at a little above ground-level, but for superior ranking warriors at special ceremonies, very long trousers were worn; these trailed on the floor and the feet were entirely enclosed within them (*14a*). The wearing of these *naga-bakama* required special skill; any change of direction had to be accompanied by sharp movements of the feet to bring the trailing portion behind the wearer, otherwise there was danger of tripping; he must also grip each leg of the trousers, pulling it up at every step to give his leg room for movement. It was possible to run in them, but this required extremely good coordination between hand and leg. Obviously this was an impracticable garment, although an imposing one; its use was a status symbol, demonstrating that its wearer had the leisure to learn to manage it, but it is also said that the rulers ordered it to be worn because it would impede anyone if he tried to make a violent attack. They were not normally worn out of doors.

Beneath the *kami-shimo*, the ordinary *kimono* was worn, with a girdle behind which the straps of the shoulder garment were inserted, and underneath that a white undergarment which showed at the neck. The swords in their scabbards were held by this girdle. The costume was completed by white *tabi*—socks with a padded sole and a division between the big toe and the smaller ones to allow for the thong of the footwear, when that was worn. The Shogun himself, and *daimyō* when not in attendance upon him, did not wear *kami-shimo*, but had luxurious garments of the normal *kimono* shape. For the rare, very grandest ceremonies, the Shogun and his entourage wore Imperial court costume, with a hat indicative of rank (*13*).

When on official journeys, mounted *samurai* wore the trousers, with a three-quarter-length *kimono*-shaped coat (*haori*) instead of the shoulder-jacket; this was held together by a tie at chest-level. A flat round hat, slightly conical, for protection against sun and rain was also standard wear. The men on foot wore a sort of breeches, drawn in at the knee, with leggings. The coat was lifted up at the back by the sword, and gave a characteristic silhouette to the *samurai* when he was on a journey (*15*).

Generally speaking, colours for *samurai* clothes were very sober, being mainly dullish blues, greys and browns, either plain or with small patterns or stripes. The shoulder-jacket and *kimono* worn beneath it normally bore the wearer's family crest, his *mon* (*14*). Trousers were lined for winter wear, unlined for summer wear, the dates for the change being fixed at the fifth day of the fifth month and the first day of the ninth month. Off-duty dress was the *kimono* without jacket or trousers. A *samurai* going to town for pleasure would often hide his face by wearing some sort of deep hat, often a rather comical basket-like affair, in order not to be recognised,

15 *Samurai* on journey

for he might well be disobeying the rules of the establishment in which he resided.

Another characteristic feature was the arrangement of the hair. The top of the head was shaved, with the hair at the back and sides gathered together into a queue, oiled, and then doubled forward over the crown, being tied where it was doubled over. The bunch of hair was trimmed off very neatly into a cleanly cut end. It was very important for the *samurai* not to have a hair out of place, and it was most embarrassing for him to have the tie become undone or cut in a sword-fight; it was even worse if the whole queue was cut off. If he was ill, he would leave the crown unshaven, and the hair would grow into a bushy mass, but he would not appear in public like this.

The greater proportion of the duties of a *samurai* were concerned with the administration of the domain to which he was attached, or, if he was part of the central organisation at Edo, with the governance of Edo itself, or of the country as a whole. The duties would vary from low-grade ones like standing guard at the castle gates to being senior councillor to a *daimyō*. If his income was derived from an actual holding of land, he would also occupy himself with this. In addition to his ordinary duties, there would of

23

course be a certain amount of obligatory ceremonial attendance. Since, therefore, most of the functions of the senior *samurai* were performed inside the castle or the government office, they might not be often seen by people of other classes, unless they were on a journey, or functioned as magistrates.

The *daimyō* in most cases had to make a periodical stay of one year every other year, in Edo. When they were on the road, they and their attendants formed a considerable spectacle: not that the populace stood and watched them go by, for the leaders of the procession shouted 'Down! Down!', and all had to prostrate themselves until the column had passed. An incident right at the end of the Tokugawa period, in 1861, when the first breaches in the seclusion of Japan had been made, illustrates the respect which was thought due on such occasions. The *daimyō* of Satsuma was returning to his domain, and when he and his retinue were nearing Yokohama, where there was already a settlement of foreign merchants, four British subjects tried to ride through the procession. The *samurai* drew their swords, and of the intruders one died and two were injured. This action of the foreigners showed what might now be seen as a shocking ignorance of the customs of the country, but the spirit of the times is indicated by the fact that the town of Kagoshima was bombarded as a reprisal, and eventually a large indemnity was paid to Britain. There were occasions when a procession might run into a different kind of trouble, especially in Kyoto: this was because a *daimyō* might be inferior in rank to an aristocrat from the Imperial Palace, although the latter was politically powerless. The appearance of such a personage in the vicinity of a procession would have caused no small confusion, with the *daimyō* having to get out of his palanquin to prostrate himself in the roadway. However, these aristocrats were in fairly impoverished circumstances and not unwilling to augment their scanty official incomes, so some were not above hinting that unless they were suitably rewarded, they might well find they had business at the critical time and place.

However, the processions normally proceeded uninterrupted, along the highways of Japan which linked Edo and the great cities and domains, the most important being the Eastern Sea Road, the Tōkaidō; it was at the time the world's busiest highway, running between what were then two of the world's largest cities, for it went from the Shogun's capital to that of the Emperor, with a

16 Ferry-boat on the Tōkaidō. In the background is the familiar silhouette of Mt Fuji

branch to the great shrine of Ise, and extending on to Osaka. Perhaps the greatest contrast between these highways and comparable ones in Europe was that there was no wheeled traffic on them. Carriages drawn by oxen were the perquisite of the Imperial court, and these would occasionally be seen around the streets and avenues of Kyoto. Some festivals employed wheeled carts in pageants, but such carts were ungainly vehicles with a fixed wheelbase, and drawn by crowds of men. Sometimes the transport of heavy loads, such as big stones for castle walls, would necessitate the use of wheeled wagons. None of these, however, affected the great highways, where travellers went on foot, or rode horses, or were carried in *kago*, palanquins like boxes suspended from a pole which the bearers bore on their shoulders. Hence no great width of roadway was required, and as there were no carts to make ruts or get stuck in them, metalling was unnecessary, for it takes extremely bad conditions to prevent men and plodding horses from getting through.

The roads were often marked by rows of trees planted close together on both sides, either tall cedars (cryptomeria) or pine

25

trees, their purpose being to define the road and prevent travellers wandering off it, and also to provide shade from sun and shelter from rain and snow. Across mountain terrain the roads would become narrower and more difficult, although well engineered. River-crossings were considerable obstacles, for there were few bridges in the country as opposed to the towns, where bridges were a common feature. Japanese rivers usually have wide beds, along which for much of the year the flow of water is divided into relatively narrow streams, at which time they did not present serious obstacles to travellers. Ferry-boats were used (*16*), and in some places porters carried people or their burdens through the water on their shoulders or on their heads. When floods came down, such crossings would become temporarily impassable and traffic be brought to an enforced halt; not for long, however, for water subsides quickly in Japan.

It would seem that the government was faced with a dilemma with regard to roads. On the one hand, good communication was necessary between Edo and the provinces, to enable officials and messengers to go speedily from one place to another; on the other, the Shogun's fear of rebellion and armed attack made him wish to restrict freedom of movement for those who were not travelling in his service. He achieved these ends partly by making the roads suitable only for foot and horse traffic, and partly by keeping in existence the system of barriers that had been in use since early times, thus using the roads themselves as controls on movement along them. It was a serious offence to try to evade the check of the officials at the barriers by taking to the fields in an attempt to bypass them, so that having to go through these barriers, of which it is estimated that more than 70 existed, had the double effect of forcing everyone to go along the roads provided, while being kept under close supervision.

An important function of this control at the barriers was to prevent the *daimyō* from moving any of his family out of Edo without permission; in particular the road-watchers had to make sure that no women moved out with the processions. Women who travelled had to carry a special certificate of authorisation which carried a full description, and they often underwent a considerable ordeal of search and interrogation at the barriers—and the higher the rank, the worse it might be. Another careful watch was kept to see that no arms, especially firearms, in sufficient quantities to

17 Post-station, with travellers and scantily clad porters arriving.
Sweaty bodies are rubbed down and horses unloaded

be used in a revolt, were taken into Edo. Restrictions extended to
the number of a *daimyō*'s attendants: for example, under the eighth
Shogun (Yoshimune, 1716–45), it was laid down that *daimyō* rated
at 200,000 *koku* or more were to have with them 120–30 foot-
soldiers and 250–300 servants and porters, while those of 100,000
koku or more could have 80 and 140–80 respectively. These numbers, when account is taken of the higher-grade *samurai* who were
also accompanying their lord, were big enough to make these
processions a considerable drain on *daimyō* resources, but not big
enough for them to constitute a threat to the central government.

The highways were divided off into stages, at each of which was
a post-station, whose duty it was to have horses and porters available for the next stage (*17*). The whole system was administered
by an office of the government, by whom the charges for use of the
service were fixed. Certain government officials were given passes
which entitled them to one horse and three men free of charge.
Daimyō on an official journey were charged a special low rate up
to a certain maximum, over which they had to pay standard

charges. They also gave notice of their plans beforehand, so that post-stations and inns could prepare what was necessary. The responsibility for providing horses and men was imposed on the local farmers, and this was just one of the ways in which they were parasitised by the *samurai*.

The *daimyō* procession was an impressive sight, with its marching men, horses and lacquered palanquins, and was made more so by the banners, spears and halberds in their decorative coverings, and other colourful objects that were borne aloft by the attendants. It formed a counterpart of the military parade as we know it in the West, and served to remind the populace of the places it passed through of the power and authority of their masters.

This authority was exercised in the towns through a system of magistrates and police. In matters of administration the local organisations in the domains followed the model of the central government in Edo, in the titles as well as in the functions of the officials, so that a description of the system in Edo will serve for the whole country.

By 1631 this system had been built up to the pattern that was to persist throughout the period. First, there were two *machi-bugyō*, 'town magistrates', who between them combined what would now be the functions of chief of police, judge and mayor. They did not, however, divide these functions between themselves, but each performed them all, being on duty for a month and off duty for the next. They were known as the North and the South. This sort of duplication was typical of the Shogun's government: in his patient preoccupation with self-preservation he tried by every means to ensure that no possible rival gained enough power to overthrow him. Each of the two magistrates was a check on the other and neither had all the resources of his office in his own hand. Both had to sign reports submitted to the government, and one result of the dual system was that individual enterprise was hampered. However, as the population of Edo increased with the tendency of people to move in from the country whenever they could, the duties of the magistrate grew more onerous, and he was glad to make full use of his month off duty to catch up with all the reports and inquiries relating to his last month on duty. Every day the magistrate on duty went to the Castle, arriving by 10 o'clock in the morning, and not leaving until about 2 o'clock. His business was with the Senior Councillors, four, or sometimes five, officials who headed the administration and were responsible to the Shogun for a wide range of affairs. He would report to them any action he had taken and receive their orders.

The post of Edo magistrate was reserved for retainers of the Shogun with the low rating of 500 *koku*, but it carried with it an allowance of 3,000 *koku*. The court rank that went with the position was equal to that of some *daimyō*, and another indication of its importance is that outstanding holders of other posts which were technically equal in status were sometimes transferred to that of Edo magistrate. His life was a busy one, for on his return to his office he would have to deal with the accumulation of paper work and other routine matters. He was not only responsible for the policing of Edo, but also dealt with civil disputes and issued travel passes. He did not, however, have to deal with *samurai* and priests, for whom there were special officials. These he would meet three times a month when, with the Senior Councillors and others, they would form a sort of high court to deal with the more serious cases.

Each magistrate had immediately under him 25 *yoriki* or assistant magistrates. They too were *samurai*, direct retainers of the Shogun, with a rating of 200 *koku*. *Yoriki* who were employed in other departments would normally receive personal appointments and not have hereditary entry into their positions, but those who worked for the Edo magistrates in practice followed their fathers and grandfathers into their profession, entering a sort of apprentice-ship at the age of 13 or thereabouts. This strong family tradition meant that the *yoriki* really knew their Edo, and they clearly formed the permanent cadre of experience and knowledge that the magistrate himself, especially when newly appointed, would rely on for the day-to-day running of his office. The *yoriki* had no hope of promotion, and lived all together in the same quarters. They thus formed a tight group, cut off by their profession and class from the townsmen with whom they were in daily contact, and also discriminated against by their superiors, for their work debarred them from entering the Castle, for fear that they would bring in contamination because of their connection with death when criminals were executed—even though the actual execution was carried out by 'non-humans'. The *yoriki* have the reputation of having been very proud of their appearance, with hair kept very neat, and always wearing two swords, with *hakama* and *haori*. It is probable that their official income was augmented by

18 *Yoriki* (*left*) and *dōshin* with a female prisoner, weeping at her misfortune

substantial gifts from *daimyō*, in return for looking after their retainers when they got drunk and disorderly.

Still lower-grade *samurai*, known as *dōshin*, 'companions', worked under the *yoriki*, and each magistrate had 120 of them (*18*). They too tended to be a closely knit hereditary group. Their income was 30 bales of rice, and they too received gifts from the *daimyō*, very often a *haori* with his crest on it, so that, since a *dōshin* might get them from several *daimyō*, he had to be careful to put on the right one when making a call at the residence of one of his benefactors. Two points should be noted about these gifts: firstly, gifts of clothing have been customary for at least 1,000 years in Japan, and until well into the present century it was still normal to give such a present to one's maid at the New Year; secondly, while the giving of such gifts might well be counted as bribery in modern times, traditional Japan was a world in which the superior and the official expected to receive them as a right, and although the receipt of a gift involved some obligation, this could immediately be forgotten in the course of official duty.

The *dōshin* maintained an individual style of dress, for although they were classed as *samurai*, they wore only one sword, and no *hakama*, and did not don the more formal dress even on ceremonial occasions, thus distinguishing themselves from the normal run of *samurai*. The *dōshin* formed the lowest rank of peace officer, and it was they that patrolled the streets of Edo, carrying as their symbol of office the *jitte*, the steel wand with a hook (*19*), the purpose of which was to catch the blade of the sword or knife of an attacker. The *dōshin* did not seek to conceal his identity, but rather resembled a uniformed officer on the beat. Edo was divided into four patrols, which meant a good deal of ground to cover. He took with him two or three assistants and called at the various watch-points that were sited in the subdivisions, manned by a representative of the local residents' association. Should there be any investigation to be made, he would send in his assistants with local men to make an arrest, not actually participating himself unless absolutely necessary. The assistants of the *dōshin* were townsfolk employed by him, and they too carried the *jitte* as their symbol of authority; however, to a large extent, they were the eyes and ears of the police, as they also acted as informers.

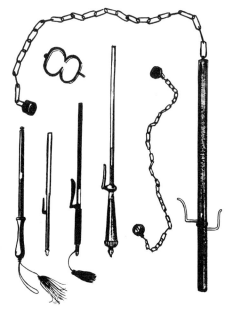

In a society like that of traditional Japan, where the principle of the inequality of human beings was accepted, every effort was made to preserve the life and safety of those of superior rank. The operation of the police force was along these lines, and most of the physical effort was put out by the assistants to the *dōshin*, and it would take a very serious incident to bring in the *yoriki*. There was a certain amount of specialised equipment available to the *dōshin* and

19 *Jitte:* various type of *jitte*, chains and handcuffs

his men for use in catching a suspect. Against the sword attack there was either the *jitte*, or a weighted steel chain (*19*) which wrapped itself round the blade. Four ladders on their sides could be used to box in a criminal, and long staves furnished with spikes and barbs could be used to inflict minor injury and wear him out, while keeping him too far away to use a sword. The first principle was that a suspect must be taken alive, and at the earliest possible moment he was secured with ropes; the tying up of prisoners was brought to a fine art of speed and security. If ever it was deemed necessary to call out the *yoriki*, he would go to the scene on horseback, with chain body armour beneath his *kimono*, and protection for hands and arms, and on his head a flat lacquered or iron-plated helmet: he would direct operations from a safe distance, and only ride in and use his lance to incapacitate the criminal if all else failed.

Once the arrest had been made, the prisoner was taken off to the office of the magistrate on duty. The Edo jail was in Denmachō, and dangerous criminals would be lodged there immediately, with a warrant from the magistrate, while less dangerous ones could be detained at the magistrate's office. With the prisoner in detention, the next stage in the process of administering justice was to persuade him to confess to his crime, for this was a prerequisite of punishment, especially when this involved execution. Basically, this was probably founded on principles of justice, to avoid punishing the innocent; confession is still, of course, preferred by the courts of many countries. (The Anglo-Saxon concept that a case should be decided on the evidence, and that a man can be expected to lie to conceal his guilt, is by no means universal.) However, the necessity for a confession implies the necessity for persuasion, if the prisoner is unwilling to confess of his own free will. Flogging, pressing with stones and water torture were among the methods available, and were no doubt put to use, just as in England it was possible to press to death prisoners who refused to plead guilty or not guilty and who therefore could not be tried. In Japan, however, the power of authority was such that few guilty men would have persisted in any denials. When the confession came, the prisoner was taken before the magistrate, and there on *shirasu*, the 'white sand' (*20*), an area before the office where the prisoners and witnesses knelt before the magistrate and gave their evidence, they heard his judgement. The 'white sand' was sym-

20 *Shirasu:* two prisoners, elaborately roped up, appear before the magistrate. Humanity allows them rough mats to kneel on

bolical of the truth of what was said there, and behind the name *shirasu* there lies, perhaps, the verb of the same pronunciation meaning 'inform'.

The most serious punishment was the death penalty, which might take several forms, and might also be followed by exposure of the corpse, as an added shame. Crimes for which death was the punishment included murder, robbery and some kinds of adultery, while burning alive was the fate of anyone convicted of arson, a much-feared crime in Japan. As an alternative to death at the executioner's hand, a *samurai* was sometimes allowed to commit suicide (*seppuku*), by which act he preserved his honour: what in fact usually happened was that immediately the knife was plunged into the left side of the abdomen, and the cut made towards the centre, the head was struck off by a blow from a friend's sword, thus cutting short the death-agony. The punishment next in severity was banishment of various degrees, from exile on some distant island down to banishment beyond ten *ri* (25 miles) from Edo, banishment from Edo, or just exclusion from the culprit's home district. Lighter punishments varied according to class. There were periods of house arrest and other restrictions on liberty. Women were sometimes punished by having their hair shaved off. Imprisonment was not a punishment; prisons existed only as places for detention while a decision was taken about guilt and sentence. Treatment in them was harsh, although a magistrate, Ōoka, who served from 1717 to 1736, and who is still remembered for his legendary ability in solving difficult cases, is credited with having brought in humanitarian reforms, especially in relation to the interrogation of prisoners. Even in prison, *samurai* were lodged separately according to whether they were superior or inferior in rank, and apart from commoners, while women were also kept in separate areas. Yet another testimony to the power of authority in Japan is that if a serious fire broke out near the jail, the prisoners were released on parole, although with the prospect of very heavy penalties if they failed to return at the specified time.

The magistrate did not deal only with criminal offences, but also had to settle disputes between individuals. It is interesting to note that the method of dealing with these involved a 'cooling-off' period, such as might be used today. On the first application to the office, the complainant would have his statement recorded, but would be sent away for a few days. If he returned then, the magistrate himself appeared, and ordered him to reconsider. If he persisted, the duty of investigating the complaint was given to a *yoriki*, who would normally carry the inquiry through, although in difficult cases it might have to go back to the magistrate, who would, in any event, deliver the final verdict.

This description of the machinery of justice in Edo serves to give some impression of the way officials worked, and of the sort of situation in which they came in contact with ordinary people. Some *samurai* would of course be in direct touch with farmers and with suppliers, but others also managed certain enterprises that would more usually be run by merchants. One outstanding example of this was the notorious gold-mine of Aikawa in the island of Sado, where folk memory has preserved tales of the harshness of the *samurai* overseers, and of the sufferings of young men forced to labour in the galleries and workings. They were in charge of an official who was equal in status to the Edo town magistrate. In other territories and domains there were other enterprises administered by *samurai*, which means that there were many who acquired experience in industrial matters: with the growth of industry after the middle of the nineteenth century, many former *samurai* were thus able to play their part in the new developments.

34

21 *Samurai* view flower-arrangement. A senior *samurai*, with two of less exalted rank, gaze at a flower-arrangement in a *toko-no-ma* (see p. 163). The figure on the right, with shaven head and fan in hand, is a Buddhist priest

In their leisure pursuits as much as in their working hours, the *samurai* were supposed to be a class apart. However, many of them spent their spare time in ways that were frowned on, since they were not encouraged to participate in any of the leisure activities of the townsfolk, things such as theatre-going and visiting the brothel districts, although it is quite clear that they did so all the same, and with the minimum of subterfuge. Many other entertainments were officially available. Of course, lower *samurai*, who might be called upon to use their fighting skill if it came to an encounter with robbers or fractious peasants, would do a certain amount of military training, and wrestling, swordsmanship, archery, riding and swimming were all practised. Upper *samurai*, while learning swordsmanship with some seriousness, pursued the study of other military sports in the same sort of spirit as they did tea-ceremony and flower-arrangement (*21*)—that is, as something more like a hobby, but learnt and practised with great seriousness and a constant search for inner significance.

All these artistic pursuits were organised into 'schools', and learnt from authorised teachers only, who taught strictly in accordance with the rules of their individual schools. Differences between them were sometimes quite small, and very often without practical importance. Even a non-artistic pursuit such as swimming was organised on a 'school' basis, each one teaching different strokes of the arms and legs, or the tactical use of various swimming styles, or horsemanship in water. The Ogasawara school was supreme in the study of polite behaviour, which included methods of greeting, posture, manners at mealtimes and so on, and also dealt with archery, a ritualised sport with considerable formality of procedure, in which as much, or even more, importance was placed upon gracefulness of movement and correctness of etiquette, as upon hitting the bull's-eye. Cruder archery competitions were sometimes indulged in, but only by lower *samurai*: one of these that is remembered took place at a temple in Kyoto, the Sanjūsangen-dō, which has a hall over 200 feet long crowded with statues. The outside gallery of this hall was used in a competition, the object of which was to shoot as many arrows as possible in a given time from one end to the other. An overhanging roof made it impossible to flight the arrows high (the beams still bear the marks where stray shots have hit), so that a strong, flat trajectory was necessary. The best performance is credited to a *samurai* in 1686, who shot 13,000 arrows, of which 8,033 reached the end of the balcony.

A more active sport for senior *samurai* was hunting. The taking of life was against the tenets of Buddhism, according to which the killing of animals might bring punishment in the next world; nevertheless, many hunted game for food, and the use of the matchlock was common, although it is unlikely that shooting was considered a sport. Quite different from this practical hunting were the large-scale expeditions by great lords. Indeed, some of the earlier Shoguns indulged in these from time to time, until they were brought to a halt by the fifth Shogun, Tsunayoshi (1680–1709). He is remembered as the 'dog' Shogun, because of his protection for these animals, occasioned by the advice received from a Buddhist priest that his childlessness was a punishment for having taken life in a previous existence: he chose the dog for his particular favour because it was the calendar sign of the year of his birth. The power of the Shogun is demonstrated by the effect that this idiosyncrasy had on the country. Some persons were even banished for killing dogs, a vast dog-pound was established in Edo for the care of strays, paid for by a special dog-tax, while the general ban on animal-killing made it difficult for the farmer to protect his crops. All this did not bring Tsunayoshi a son, however, and he was succeeded by a nephew, who immediately brought the dog-favouring edicts to an end. The Shogun Yoshi-mune (1716–45) was an energetic instigator of reforms, and also endeavoured to bring the *samurai* back to their early simplicity by encouraging them to take physical exercise. In particular he favoured hunting, and in the list of nicknames of Shoguns he is called the 'falcon' Shogun. On his hawking expeditions he was accompanied by a large retinue, and the victims were cranes and other wild birds. He also revived the deer- and boar-hunts that had been favourite sports of some of his predecessors: these were decidedly unsporting affairs in which the game was driven towards the 'hunters', who dispatched them with arrows or gunshot from the safety of horseback.

An anecdote preserved in the diary (1692) of a *samurai* in Nagoya reveals the standard of values at the time.

> The lord of Iyo (in Shikoku) lost a favourite hawk, and sought for it throughout his domain. One day a certain farmer went out to tend his fields, while his wife stayed at home with her weaving. A hawk flew in and perched on her loom. The wife took her shuttle and struck the bird, which straightway died. The farmer returned home and was told by his wife how a beautifully marked bird had settled on her loom, how she had struck at it without intending to kill it, but how the bird had unfortunately died. Her husband looked at it and saw it was a hawk. He was greatly alarmed, for he knew that the lord was searching for such a bird. With much trepidation he told the village headman about what had happened, and the occurrence was reported to the bailiff. The latter, in great anger, had the husband and wife bound, and taken before his lord for trial. The lord, too, was enraged, and had the wife crucified, but pardoned the husband because he was not at home at the time in question.

The story goes on to relate that when the husband went to pray for his wife, he found that she was still alive, and the lord, hearing this, had her taken down. She claimed to have been saved by a protective deity. The *samurai* who noted all this did not seem to

22 Puppet-show in a *daimyō's* residence

find the treatment of the woman surprising; it was her return to
life that astonished him.

However, the hunting Yoshimune was exceptional, as the
Shogun did not normally participate in active sports. Their
amusements were usually much less energetic, and they would be
spectators rather than participants. For example, they and the
daimyō supported *sumō*, a form of wrestling, which already had a
long history of popularity in Japan, as well as the patronage of the
Imperial court. Another source of entertainment was the drama.
Samurai were discouraged from going to the theatres where the
merchants formed the audiences, but this did not prevent *daimyō*
and others from summoning companies or individual performers
to their residences. The Shogun would have *nō* plays given in the
Castle, and would allow the townsfolk to see one of the performances. Surviving records show that the lords of Tottori were
great patrons of the *nō* when they were doing their obligatory
attendance upon the Shogun. The *daimyō* himself played the chief

role in many of the plays, which were put on to entertain his guests, often other *daimyō*, at parties, in the latter part of the seventeenth century. Actors and musicians were paid with money or clothing, and, if asked to travel, were given special allowances and an escort. *Kabuki* and the puppet-plays were also to be seen in the residence, but less often than the *nō*, the puppets being specially for the diversion of the lower ranks of the household.

Another, and much more personal, record is a diary left by a lord known as Matsudaira, Governor of Yamato (a province he had nothing to do with, his title being a purely nominal one granted by the Imperial court), who died in Edo in his fifty-fourth year, in 1695. He was interested in artistic pursuits and entertainments of all sorts, including calligraphy, perfume-discrimination, *nō* plays and their comic interludes (*kyōgen*), puppet and *kabuki* plays, painting, poetry of all kinds, dancing, wrestling and hunting. He was in almost daily touch with events in the theatre district, often sending men there to see performances and report on them, or interrogating those who had passed by the theatres about what new signs were up and what the gossip was. His circle of acquaintances was apparently composed of admirers of the puppet-plays in particular, for he often mentions going to parties at other mansions and being entertained by famous performers, besides putting on similar performances for his own guests (*22*).

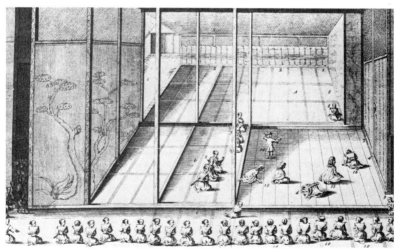

23 Kaempfer at the Shogun's court

It might be a little cynical to suggest that the rarest entertainment for the Shogun's court was the annual visit from the head (or Captain) of the Dutch factory (trading post) in Nagasaki. This was seen partly as a favour to allow him to escape for a few weeks from his narrow quarters, and partly, of course, as an opportunity to acquire some curious foreign gifts. In 1691 a German doctor, Engelbert Kaempfer, was physician to the Dutch, and went with them to Edo. He has left a vivid description of his journey, and of his audiences with the Shogun. The first of these was formal, but, says, Kaempfer, for their second audience they were

conducted through several dark galleries. Along all these several galleries there was one continual row of lifeguard men, and nearer to the Imperial apartments followed, in the same row, some great officers of the Crown, who lined the front of the hall of the audience, clad in their garments of ceremony, bowing their heads, and sitting on their heels. The hall of audience was just as I represented it in the Figure hereunto annexed (23). It consisted of several rooms, looking towards a middle place, some of which were laid open towards the same, others covered by screens and lattices. Some were of 15 mats, others of 18, and they were a mat higher or lower, according to the quality of the persons seated in the same. The middle place had no mats at all, they having been taken away, and was consequently the lowest, on whose floor, covered with neat varnished boards, we were commanded to sit down. The Emperor [i.e. the Shogun] and his Imperial Consort sat behind the lattices on our right. . . . By Lattices, I mean hangings made of reed, split exceeding thin and fine and covered on the back with a fine transparent silk, with openings about a span broad, for the person behind to look through. For ornament's sake, and the better to hide the persons standing behind, they are painted in divers figures, though otherwise it would be impossible to see them at a distance, chiefly when the light is taken off behind. The Emperor himself was in such an obscure place, that we should scarce have known him to be present, had not his voice discovered him, which was yet so low, as if he purposely intended to be there incognito. Just before us, behind other lattices, were the Princes of the blood, and the Ladies of the Empress. I took notice, that pieces of paper were put between the reeds in some parts of the Lattices, to make the openings wide, in order to have a better and easier sight. I counted about thirty such papers, which made me conclude, that there was about that number of persons sitting behind. . . . We were commanded to sit down, having first made our obeysances after the Japanese manner, creeping and bowing our heads to the ground,

24 The Shogun attended by ladies-in-waiting (wax models). Behind the tasselled doors in this private apartment in the Nijō Castle an armed guard was always on duty

towards that part of the Lattices, behind which the Emperor was. The chief Interpreter sat himself a little forward, to hear more distinctly, and we took our places on his left hand all in a row.

In the ensuing conversation the Shogun's words were directed to the President of the Council of State, who repeated them to the interpreter, for transmission to the visitors. Kaempfer remarks:

I fancy that the words, as they flow out of the Emperor's mouth are esteemed too precious and sacred for an immediate transit into the mouth of persons of low rank.

After interrogation about the outside world and on medical matters, the foreigners were ordered by the Shogun to

take off our Cappa, or Cloak, being our garment of ceremony, then to stand upright, that he might have a full view of us; again to walk, to stand still, to compliment each other, to dance, to jump, to play the drunkard, to speak broken Japanese, to read Dutch, to paint, to sing, to put our cloaks on and off. Mean while we obeyed the Emperor's commands in the best manner we could, I joined to my dance a love-song in High German. In this manner, and with

41

innumerable such other apish tricks, we must suffer ourselves to contribute to the Emperor's and the Court's diversion. . . . Having been thus exercised for a matter of two hours, though with great apparent civility, some servants came in and put before each of us a small table with Japanese victuals, and a couple of Ivory sticks, instead of knives and forks. We took and eat some little things, and our old chief Interpreter, though scarce able to walk, was commanded to carry away the remainder for himself.

Kaempfer was a trained observer and one can accept his description as accurate. It is possible that the mats were removed in the area of floor in which the Dutchmen appeared because they wore shoes. The Japanese always left their outdoor footwear at the entrance, and from then on went either barefoot or wearing *tabi*, the divided socks—unless they were on urgent official business, such as making an arrest, in which case they would go straight in, thus increasing, incidently, the psychological shock of the irruption.

It sounds as if Kaempfer in this unofficial audience penetrated

25 The Shogun's ladies exercising with the halberd

26 The Shogun's ladies at their toilet

as far as the semi-private domestic quarters, one of the three main
divisions of the Edo Castle: the 'front', where business was conducted, the 'middle interior', referred to above, and the 'great
interior', which was the women's quarters (*24*). The organisation of
the latter is believed to have been modelled on that of the Chinese
court. In the Edo 'great interior' only very few men were allowed
in—the Shogun himself, some senior counsellors, doctors and
priests. The women had ranks reminiscent of those of the government, with a jealously preserved hierarchy, and they were even
prepared to fight if necessary, being trained in the use of the
halberd (*25*). They were recruited from the daughters of direct
retainers, and started their apprenticeship at about the age of 12.
It was, of course, a great honour to serve in this establishment, and
usually it was a job for life, although occasionally a Shogun would
release a concubine of whom he had grown tired, giving her in
marriage to one of his retainers, just as he might take in some
beauty at a later age than was usual. He had a consort (Kaempfer's
Empress), whom he would have married for political reasons, but
nobody would have expected him not to have other women—
Ienari, the eleventh Shogun (1787–1838), is reported to have had
15 concubines and 24 less regularly chosen companions. The
formula used by the Shogun, indicating his choice for the night,

was for him to ask one of the senior women: 'What is that girl's name?', which would set the machinery of preparation in motion.

A great deal of the time of these women was spent in dressing and making-up (26), since their costume and appearance at their various duties in attendance on their master was governed by the strictest etiquette. Then all the polite attainments—flower-arrangement, tea-ceremony, incense-discrimination—had to be practised, and there was a certain amount of leisure for things like playing poem-cards, or cherry-blossom viewing in the Castle grounds. Perhaps the ever-present occupation was the pursuit of intrigue, back-biting and jealousy inescapable from the circum-stances they lived in. Occasionally there were intrigues of another sort, and one in particular is worth recording for the light it throws on the less conventional activities of the Tokugawa ladies. One of the inmates of the harem, as it might justifiably be called, by name Ejima, had acquired a fairly elevated position, and it was one of her duties to deal with the tradespeople who were appointed to furnish goods to the Shogun's household. Either directly, or through the intermediary of a doctor in the Castle, she was approached by certain merchants who wished to join the favoured circle, and as part of the inducement she was taken to the Nakamura theatre, and introduced to one of its actors, Ikushima. Accounts of the incident vary in detail—she may even have smuggled him into her room at the Castle—but they had an affair, Ikushima's part in which may have been due to a substantial bribe from the merchants involved rather than from his true senti-ments. They were observed, reports sent to the authorities, and in 1714 Ejima was sent into exile (her punishment might have been worse had she not been protected by the Shogun's favourite), as were Ikushima and other members of the theatre. Ejima's brother, however, was condemned to death, not necessarily because he had anything to do with the scandal, but because a family was respon-sible for its members. The four theatres that existed in Edo at the time were closed; three of them were allowed later to reopen, but the Nakamura went out of business for ever. There were several elements in the incident that were particularly repugnant to the government, among them being the intrusion of another man into the Shogun's sexual domain, and the involvement of members of the *samurai* class with merchants and the power of their money.

The disparity of status between men and women among the

27 Japanese and Chinese styles of writing. Both these inscriptions read the same—*Fujiwara Mitsushige hitsu* 'drawn by Fujiwara Mitsushige'—but (a) is in the flowing Japanese style, and (b) in the square Chinese style

(a)   (b)

samurai was far greater than in the lower classes. The official wife was always chosen for reasons of policy, never of affection, and in fact it is clearly stated in the various *samurai* codes that such an important thing as marriage should not be undertaken lightly, but only after serious consideration of all the factors involved. The humbler the *samurai* the better the treatment he gave his wife, while those of the *daimyō*, who had to spend their whole time in Edo, were particularly unfortunate, though they were not lacking in material comfort. The moral standards required of each side were vastly different: the *samurai* demanded the strictest fidelity from their womenfolk, but, of course, were completely free from such restrictions themselves. A mistress or concubine could not, by edict, become an official spouse, although the frequency with which such edicts were published suggests that perhaps some *samurai* became sentimentally attached to the extent of wishing to marry a mistress.

The education of a woman was directed towards making her of

28 The Shogun Yoshimune in full regalia

use to the men to whom she owed her loyalty—her father, her husband, her eldest son—and then to women such as the lord's wife and daughters, and her own mother-in-law. There were no schools for the daughters of *samurai*; they learned in their homes, from the women round them, the practical skills of housekeeping and being a good wife, and from visiting teachers the social graces of traditional ritual, as in flower-arrangement and the tea-ceremony, and of dance, song and the playing of the *koto*, the horizontal harp. They would learn to write, in the flowing Japanese style rather than the stiff Chinese calligraphy, and to read the classical Japanese novels and poetry, even though some moralists condemned the eleventh-century *Tale of Genji*, now recognised to be the masterpiece of Japanese novel-writing, as liable to put licentious thoughts into chaste heads.

For boys, things were quite different, but an account of their schools, and what was taught in them must be preceded by some explanation of the nature of the Japanese language and its relation to Chinese. Japanese is, in vocabulary and grammar, quite different from Chinese, but it had no native form of writing. The Chinese language was imported along with various other aspects of Chinese civilisation and the Buddhist religion, in the sixth and seventh centuries. Later, Chinese characters were used to write Japanese. However, the Chinese language, for the writing of which they were developed, has, for example, no grammatical endings to its words, and gets its effects purely by combinations of these characters, which are intrinsically expressions of meaning; whereas Japanese has complicated grammatical endings, and to express these, and other elements, it had to use Chinese characters purely for their sound. The dual system thus arose of expressing a Japanese word either by a character which had the approximate meaning required, or by the characters used phonetically, or by a combination of the two. In the course of time the characters used phonetically developed into a relatively simple syllabary (in which a symbol expresses a vowel or combination of consonant and vowel), and Japanese thus came to be written in a mixture of characters and phonetic symbols. When writing Japanese, one tended to use a cursive style, that is, one in which the characters and symbols assumed abbreviated and flowing forms. When writing Chinese, one used square characters, comparable to block capitals in the alphabet (27).

One of the fundamental aims at the schools for *samurai* boys was the teaching of how to read Chinese texts, using the conventional devices, such as reading the characters in a different order from that in which they appeared in the text, and adding grammatical endings, so that they sounded like a very stilted Japanese. The texts were the Chinese classics and works of Confucian ethics, and their content formed the typical *samurai* mind, with the value it placed on loyalty to superiors, the need for decorum, and a strong feeling of superiority to those who were not *samurai*. The teaching of calligraphy was also of great importance, and lastly, the rules of etiquette—how to behave towards one's superiors according to their rank, as well as manners to be observed at mealtimes, correct posture and so on—were inculcated, together with a grounding in the use of weapons.

Most domains had schools attached to them, attended by all except the sons of top-ranking *samurai*, such as *daimyō*, and of the

Shogun himself; for them private teaching was provided. The organisation of schools varied from place to place, and, in some, attendance was compulsory, but usually it was not. Education could start at the age of six, and could go on, in the case of gifted students, to the thirties, by which age they would be doing some teaching of younger boys. Most of the instruction, however, was by professional teachers. The general pattern was that the boys had short sessions of individual instruction or testing, with longer periods for practice and preparation. One factor operating here was the desire to avoid lowering a pupil's dignity—making him lose face—in the presence of his comrades, who might, in any case, be of inferior status. There was also a programme of lectures on general matters. Although there was a system of examinations, with prizes for the successful, care was taken not to encourage competition, which was considered undesirable in persons who were to live in a strictly regulated class society. In fact, it might not be unfair to say that if boys did well at school it was because they liked learning, and valued the honour of receiving awards from above, for there was little material benefit to be gained, since inefficiency or ignorance were not likely to deprive one of one's post. It is true that the central government did have a system of salaries for certain posts that it had to fill, but they were very few in number, and not open to those on 'outside lord' domains. It was different for a woman, who could be dismissed by her husband if she did not match up to his requirements, so that she had a spur to learn her job thoroughly, but no schools to teach her.

By their early training then, the *samurai* learned to be respectful and loyal to his superiors, to conduct himself with dignity and decorum, to judge conduct by standards of morality and never by worldly success, and to act justly to those beneath him. Although the majority of them got on quietly with the work that came their way, using precedent in making decisions, and sometimes acquiring considerable administrative skills (which were to be of great use when the whole system collapsed in the 1860s, and many former *samurai* turned to the task of modernising Japan), their rigid class-consciousness and their certainty of their high place in society made them into some of the most stiff-necked and intransigent men the world has known. When their ancestors were fighting the civil wars that preceded the seventeenth century, they tended to be practical soldiers, with a flexible professional approach to life, which took account of the fact that a victory today might be followed by a defeat tomorrow, and that the more heads one took on the battlefield, the greater the reward from one's general, provided one was on the winning side and survived. Their descendants in the Tokugawa period knew that their status would not change, but were ever obliged to underline their position by the different attitudes they adopted to superiors and inferiors, demonstrated by the intricate linguistic system by which respect or lack of it was expressed. Even today in Japanese one can use different styles of language for the respect-worthy persons one talks about or addresses, and for the humbler persons that the speaker and his group represent. The *samurai* had a wider range, for he used to inferiors a language that underlined his superiority and their low station.

It was a constant fear of all grades of *samurai* that commoners would seek to rise above their allotted place in the scheme of things, and towards them they showed a particularly unbending attitude, typified by the strutting walk and haughty glare that swept all from their path as they went by. Their arrogance was backed by their swords, less used, perhaps, than modern films would have one believe, but all the same some of the most formidable cutting weapons ever devised: they had razor-sharp blades and a weight of metal that found little to resist them in a human body, and a commoner knew better than to offer an impertinence to a *samurai*, for he risked his life in doing so. If the *samurai* were the only class that had the right to wear two swords, equally they were the only ones with two names, being the possessors of an honoured family name as well as their personal ones. Everything possible emphasised their privileged position in a society designed to maintain it, and in which the cleavage was between the *samurai* on the one hand, and all the rest—farmers, merchants and skilled workers —on the other.

Two examples of *mon*, Japanese family crests. On the left is a mandarin orange and on the right a three-leaf hollyhock

3

The Farmers

The main function of the farmer was to grow rice for the *samurai*; but the growing of rice, although it was his most important occupation, was not his sole one. Rice, as it is grown in Japan and in the other great production areas of Asia, requires absolutely flat fields which can be flooded at the appropriate moment; these fields are surrounded by low embankments to prevent the water escaping. Plains are not very extensive, but where they exist, such as behind Tokyo, behind Nagoya, and around Nara, fields can be fairly large and regular in pattern; the more characteristic fields, however, occur up the valleys and hill-sides, where fields are cut out in terraces, and here they are much more irregular than in the plains because they have to be adapted to the terrain.

Since all of the three islands of old Japan (i.e. not counting Hokkaidō) were divided into domains or directly held territories, it was necessary to grow rice throughout the country, even though

29 Ploughing

30 Sprouting rice before sowing. The farmhouse has a small bamboo grove behind it

there were many marginal districts where climate or terrain made this difficult. Other characteristic units in a farming village, apart from the flat rice-fields, were the dry fields on which other crops might be grown—wheat, millet, and other grains, cotton, tobacco, hemp and sweet potato—and also the permanently planted areas where, according to region, there would be oranges, grapes, mulberry plants, tea or bamboos. Scattered fruit trees, such as persimmons, plums and apricots might be found; some crops, like beans, were even grown on the embankments between the fields. In more favoured districts the rice-fields would support an off-season crop (that could be grown and harvested before the land was needed for the rice), such as rape, grown for the oil extracted from the seed.

Life in the country, especially in the north, is regulated by the seasons, which are clearly marked in most parts of Japan. Nature and the seasons are a constant theme in Japanese poetry, for the

Japanese are very sensitive to their manifestations. Spring, which is misty and mild, sees the blooming of the plum, followed by the cherry; with its gentle rain it is the season of renewal, heralded by the fresh green of new leaves, while a little later the falling of the cherry blossom adds a touch of melancholy to the scene with the reminder that, just as the flowers are scattered in the breeze, so also is human life doomed to end. Summer, although an ideal growing season for rice, is unpoetical, a season to be endured rather than enjoyed, for it is hot and sultry, and brings heavy rains followed by typhoons. Autumn, on the contrary, is a most welcome season, with its clear dry weather affording relief after the heat and heavy rains; in the country it is, of course, the time of harvest, but it is also the time of change and decay, and so poetically the most characteristically Japanese of the seasons, with signs of impermanence everywhere, symbolised by the momentary dew on the now scarlet maple leaf. Although winter is of short duration and rather dry in the south, over much of the country Japan is just a snow-covered landscape in this season; the Japanese cope valiantly with the cold weather, for their houses do not provide much protection against it.

The farmer in Japan has therefore the advantage of weather that, whatever its other faults, is reasonably predictable, so that agricultural operations seldom have to wait upon it. This does not mean that there are not occasional droughts, while the occurrence and precise course of typhoons in late summer cannot be foreseen. The first act in the cycle of rice-production was to prepare the nursery bed in May. For various reasons, rice was not sown directly in the

31 Sowing rice. The nursery-bed is divided by ropes to help even distribution of the seed

32 Rice-planting. Men bring seedlings from the nursery-bed, and young women plant them out

place where it was to grow, but plants were reared in a nursery bed for later transplanting. This method, economical of seed, concentrates the seedlings in a small area where they can be easily supervised, and allows any secondary crops in the main fields a longer time to mature. The preparation of the bed involved ploughing up the area (29) if beasts were available—horses being more common in eastern Japan and oxen in the west—or digging by hand, adding manure and producing a smooth area. Water for the fields either came by gravity-fed channels, led into and from the fields by arrangements of water-gates or bamboo tubes, or, in flat areas, it was raised by mechanical means, water-wheels if the flow was fast enough, tread-wheels or other devices where it was not (33).

The seed, saved from last year's crop, was often sprouted before sowing (30), being soaked, in the straw bales in which it was stored, by suspension in a pond, then spread in the sun. It was scattered on the bed from the banks and sank to the surface of the

33 Three methods of raising water—by cranks, treadmill and Archimedean screw. Note the embanking above and the girl bringing refreshments

soil (*31*). Forty days was required for it to grow to sufficient size for planting out—something like 12 inches overall.

The main fields were prepared by ploughing or digging, to get rid of any stubble remaining and to turn in weeds and manure in the form of vegetable compost, ashes, mud from ditches, and so on. If the field was not already naturally flooded, this cultivation might be done before the water was brought in, but at all events the field was flooded before the planting. This was one of the great occasions of the year. It was organised as a communal operation, with persons from a group of farms co-operating. The actual planters were usually young women, partly perhaps because of their dexterity, but mainly from a traditional feeling that their potential fertility as child-bearers would transfer itself to the rice. They worked in line—usually backwards, but sometimes forwards —across the field, pushing the roots of the plants into the soft mud at regular intervals (*32*). Plants were taken from the beds by more experienced workers, to avoid root-damage, tied into bundles and thrown into the fields so that the transplanters could pick them up. An important duty of the owner of the field was the provision of

34 A procession of villagers with torches, banging drums and bells, blowing conch-shells, and bearing an effigy of Sanemori, makes its way to the shrine, indicated by the characteristic gateway (*torii*)

food, and pictures of rice-planting nearly always include a young
girl loaded with trays and carrying liquid refreshment. The work
is very arduous, done with bent backs and requiring speed,
rhythm and endurance; in many places songs were sung accompanied by music and dancing on the embankments, as much to
relieve the tedium of the planting and provide a rhythmical
stimulus as to celebrate the joy of restarting the crop cycle. Some
of this music is very old, and became incorporated in the begin-
nings of the classic *nō* drama, centuries before 1600.

With the planting completed, the fields have now their most
characteristic appearance, covered in water reflecting the sky and
dotted by the green of the young rice plants. These grow steadily
until the all-over colour is a light green, and the water is hidden
by the plants and a film of water-weeds. Frogs breed in the fields,
and the air is full of their croaking. Hoeing between the rows must
be done to keep the weeds in check, the embankments need attention to prevent them crumbling, and the water-level has to be

35 Threshing. Sheaves are brought in by men and an ox, and hung
on racks to dry. Some grain is threshed with flails, while women
heckle rice. In the shelter two men work, with ropes, a machine
separating grain from husks

36 Heckling rice. Two ways of stripping the rice grain from the ears

maintained. This is the time when disputes about water would arise, especially if rainfall was below normal. One farmer might divert water into his own field, or open up a channel from a higher field than his own, and such actions would lead to bitter recriminations.

Generally speaking, during the time from planting to harvesting, rice does not require a great deal of attention. There were years, however, in which insect damage was heavy, heavy enough virtually to destroy the crop in some regions. Round about the end of July was the time when the infestations were likely to build up, and this was an anxious time. Various remedies were available, some using fumigation and catching by hand the winged form of the pest. One very effective treatment was apparently discovered in Kyūshū, which averted the worst ravages; it consisted of heating together whale-oil and vinegar, and spraying the growing plants. It was found that whale-oil could be replaced by other oils, and the practice spread to the whole of Japan. The liquid was scattered over the plants with straw brooms. Another treatment depended upon quite other principles, those of magic. Straw images of the larvae that caused the damage, or of human figures representing either an evil spirit or a good spirit who was requested to take away the insects with him, were paraded around the fields, the villagers bearing blazing torches and beating upon bells and drums (*34*). The images were cast into a river to be washed away, or burned or otherwise disposed of. When the effigy is human, it is often called Sanemori, after a warrior who died in the great civil wars of the twelfth century. More straightforward recourse to religion would be occasioned by a shortage of rain at a critical time, when prayers were offered, either to implore the gods that were thought to give rain, or to appease some hostile spirit that was withholding it.

In late August or September the flowers opened on the rice, and it was ready for harvesting in October or early November, depending upon the latitude and local climate. Normally winter does not come to Japan until late in December, so that November is still autumnal, with calm weather and colourful leaves in the woods, and the frosts that would be fatal to rice have not yet started. During autumn, while the crop is ripening, the water in the fields is allowed to evaporate or drain away, so that the ground is usually firm by the time reaping begins. The harvesting was done by hand, with sickles, and the rice was cut low down, to leave long stalks; it was tied into bundles or small sheaves, and if necessary was stored by piling in circular stacks or hung head downwards to dry from ropes strung between trees. In the earlier part of the Tokugawa period the grain was stripped (the technical term is 'rippled' or 'heckled') by pulling the plants between two sticks, or even by striking them against the top of an open tub. Later in the period there developed a toothed device, through which they were drawn to separate the grains (*36*). Flails, like those used in the West, with a hinged piece of wood at the head of a pole, existed in Japan at the time, but they were probably used for threshing other grains such as barley or wheat rather than rice (*35*). The grains which had been stripped from the plants were next winnowed by being scooped up in flat baskets and thrown in the air. What was left was the brown rice with the husk still on, known as *genmai*, 'black rice'. It was at this stage that sufficient was selected as seed for sowing next year, and put aside. It was also as *genmai* that most of the rice went to the *samurai*, after it had been sorted over by hand, and packed into barrel-shaped bales, which were made of rice-straw and of double thickness to minimise spillage.

The other crops were grown either in special fields, round the

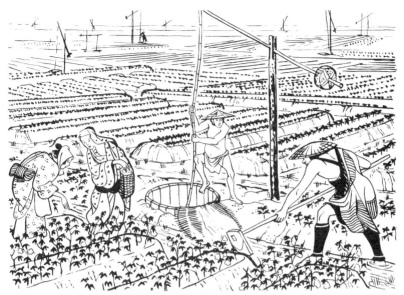

37 Growing cotton required much water, and the fields are dotted
with wells

edges of the rice-fields, or in raised strips in these fields. The grains
other than rice included some that closely resembled wheat and
barley as they are known today (used to supplement rice as the
staple food, and in the manufacture of some products, such as soy
sauce). Bread was not known outside Nagasaki, where wheat-flour
was used in making *kasutera*, the sponge-cake which presumably
came in with the Portuguese, since its name seems to be derived
from *castella*. Millet was also used to supplement rice, and also to
make cakes and dumplings. Buckwheat was eaten in the form of
noodles. All these were grown in dry fields, in intervals of work
on rice.

These supplementary crops were manured with human excre-
ment and urine, ladled out of the cess-pits that directly underlay
the holes in the floor that served as privies. The handling of this
material in the towns was a large-scale operation, with boats
transporting it to where it was needed. In the country it had to be
transported over shorter distances, and could be carried in wooden
buckets slung on a pole. Roads passing through villages would
have tubs conveniently placed for the use of passers-by, so that

nothing should be wasted. Before being applied to the plants, this manure was normally diluted with water, and it was then poured round the roots of the crops, or trees. Noses could not afford to be too sensitive. A more serious drawback to its use was the spread of some diseases; in particular, human intestinal worms flourished in these conditions. It was not used for the general manuring of rice, which depended upon dry material worked in when the fields were prepared, and on matter brought in solution or suspension by the water-supply.

Other crops included fruit such as plums (usually small, more like damsons, and eaten after being pickled), persimmons (a fruit tending to be astringent unless fully ripe, when it glows golden in the autumn sun, and becoming very sweet when sun-dried), pears (spherical in shape and crisp in texture) and oranges (small tangerine-like *mikan*). Usually these were grown for eating on the farm, but in some places, such as the Kii province for oranges, and Kōshū for grapes (grown only for eating as fruit), land was set aside for their cultivation on a commercial scale. Tea was grown as individual bushes scattered around the farm, as well as in the specialist regions, like Uji to the south of Kyoto. Certain vegetables, like the giant radish and lotus roots, were produced partly for commerce, while the woods would be searched for mushrooms, wild fruits and green herbs, the first sprouting of bracken being a considerable delicacy.

Certain regions had specialised crops for industrial use. For example, the north-west corner of the island of Shikoku, the province of Awa, produced indigo for dyeing. This was a plant that was reared in nursery beds and transplanted, being harvested just before flowering. It was cut up fine, and sun-dried, the product being then fermented in a little water. For commerce it was then ground down and worked into balls about the size of billiard balls.

Plants giving material for textiles included hemp, used extensively for outer clothing, like the *hakama* of warriors, and grown widely in Japan, especially where the climate was more rigorous. The growing of cotton (*37*) seems to have started in the late sixteenth century, although it had been imported from China for some centuries. It was not an easy crop and required considerable attention from the farmers. It needs plenty of water during the growing season, but dry weather after flowering, and this latter requirement can be met only in the coastal areas round the Inland Sea, and in fact the main producing region seems to have been round the city of Osaka. It was often grown in conjunction with rice, either by an alternation of crops when the fields could be completely drained, or by building up raised beds in the rice-fields. The picking of the cotton was largely done by women. The clothing of farmers was restricted by decree to hemp and cotton, so that a good deal of the production was reserved for home use, spinning and weaving being two of the more usual occupations of the womenfolk.

The third widely used textile material was silk, which, although they produced it, the farmers were not allowed to use. By far the greater proportion of silk thread came from worms reared in special rooms, very often in the upper floor of farmhouses, rather than from cocoons collected from outside, where the silkworms had been feeding on trees. Silk-rearing was virtually restricted to the main island. The normal procedure was that eggs were kept in a cool place over the winter, adhering naturally to the paper on which the moths had been induced to lay them the season before. The mulberry trees that provided the food for the grubs were every year cut down nearly to ground-level so that shoots grew out in spring, which produced particularly large and succulent leaves from the middle of May. When he saw that the leaves would be available in time, the farmer or his womenfolk would bring out the eggs from the cool store, and spread out the papers on which they still stuck in the special rooms, which have to be dry, with fresh air and no direct sun. As the larvae emerged, they were transferred to a bed of chopped leaves, either individually by hand, or by some device such as spreading the leaves on a sheet of paper in which holes were made, and covering the eggs with this: the larvae soon found their way through the holes on to the leaves. It was very important to keep the food-stuff clean and fresh. The larvae were provided with up to five meals a day and their beds had to be cleaned at least once during this time, which lasts a little over a month and in the course of which the larvae cast their skins four times; then they spin their cocoons, attaching themselves to twigs or straws provided for them.

It takes three or four days for the spinning of the cocoon to be completed, and it is left for another week or so to mature: it then consists of an outer covering of loose silk which cannot be reeled

38 Farm implements: (1) straw hat and raincoat (2) frame for carrying loads on back (3) pattens for walking in rice-fields (4) tobacco-cutting block (5) spade-ploughs, pushed with foot (6) heckling frame (7) bamboo tubes for insertion into rice-bales to sample contents (8) food-boxes (9) mattocks and sickles (10) water-bottle (11) bird-scarer (12) screen for sieving grain. The other tools are easily identifiable

off as a single thread, but is used as floss or wadding for padding quilted clothing. The bulk of the cocoon forms a length of silk, perhaps 500 yards long. The best cocoons are picked out for breeding, the moths being allowed to develop and make their way out of their integuments to mate and deposit their eggs for the next season. In the process of breaking out, they split the silk, and the cocoons that are to be used for thread do not reach this stage, but are killed by being exposed to the sun or immersed in hot water. Before the thread is unreeled, the cocoon is soaked in warm water, which frees the outer layers and makes it possible for the end of the thread to be discovered. The various sorts of yarn used to make different varieties of fabric are made by spinning together the threads from varying numbers of cocoons.

The care of the silkworms took up a great deal of time and energy on the part of the women whose duty this normally was. It is typical of the thrift of the farmers that hardly any of the silk was discarded—even ill-shaped or diseased cocoons could be used for some purpose, even though the thread could not be cleanly reeled off.

All the occupations that have been described so far were concentrated in the summer months. Except in cases where a back-season crop was grown, there was no agricultural activity from November to April. There were, of course, many other things to be done, such as the collection of fuel, in the form of dried leaves and wood, and of fodder for any beasts that were kept, as well as the usual winter chores of making and mending tools and equipment. Spinning and weaving were the chief productive activities, along with certain other handicrafts, and some brewing of *sake*, the alcoholic liquor prepared from rice and drunk on festive occasions.

Ihara Saikaku, an eighteenth-century novelist, included a story in his collection, *The Japanese family storehouse*, about a farmer who made good: he was considerably idealised, being given credit for improvements that were certainly not the product of just one man's brain, but the story demonstrates the reward that virtue might bring. In typically Saikaku fashion, the second half of this story shows the farmer's son, after his death, squandering his fortune and reducing the family to penury. The following is a paraphrase of the first part of this little tale:

> There was a small farmer called Kusuke who scraped a wretched living in the village of Asahi in Yamato. He worked his land by his own efforts, for he had no oxen, and his wife toiled from first light at her loom, weaving hempen cloth. In many an autumn he had measured out the one and two-tenths *koku* of taxation-rice, and until the age of over 50 he carried out the usual rituals at the New Year, hung sardine heads and holly at his tiny windows like everyone else, and threw beans down as a protection against the invisible demons that come around. One year he gathered the beans together again, and on impulse sowed one of them in a piece of waste land. That summer it produced a mass of stalks green with leaves, and in the autumn there ripened more than a double handful of beans. These he sowed along the water-channels between his rice-fields, and each year without fail he harvested them. The yield increased until after ten years it reached 88 *koku*. With the proceeds of this he had a great lantern built to lighten the darkness on the Hase highway: it still shines and is known as the 'bean lantern'.

All things gradually accumulate, and man's greatest desires some-times come to fruition. Kusuke continued to work in the same spirit to increase the prosperity of his household. He acquired more land for rice and other crops, and in time became a big farmer. At the proper time he manured his fields and removed weeds, and let in water, so that the ears of his rice ripened plump and full, and the flowers of his cotton plants looked like flights of butterflies. If his prosperity was greater than that of other men, it was not only by chance, but because he worked unceasingly, morning and evening, hard enough to wear out his spade and hoe. He was a man of great ingenuity, who did much for the good of mankind. He made the rake with its rows of iron teeth, and there was nothing of more use to men for breaking up the soil. He also introduced the Chinese Winnower and the Thousand Koku Sieve. The work of threshing corn by hand took a great deal of time, and he invented an implement with a row of bamboo spikes, so that whereas two men had been needed to thresh his crop, now one could do it without great effort. He also developed a device whereby a woman could prepare many times more cotton for spinning in a day than before. He bought snowy mountains of cotton, employed many workers, and sent countless bales to Edo. In four or five years he acquired great wealth, and became one of the most notable cotton-dealers in his province.

The authorities would doubtless have approved highly of Kusuke, exemplifying as he did thrift and continuous activity by the farming community, but their characteristically contemptuous attitude to the major section of the population, on whom, after all, they depended directly for their whole livelihood, is expressed very clearly in some extracts (which are quoted by G. Sansom in his *A History of Japan, 1615-1867*, London, 1964) of an ordinance that was issued to villages in 1649:

> Farm work must be done with the greatest diligence. Planting must be neat, all weeds must be removed, and on the borders of both wet and dry fields beans or similar food-stuffs are to be grown, however small the space.
> Peasants must rise early and cut grass before cultivating the fields. In the evening they are to make straw rope and straw bags, all such work to be done with great care.
> They must not buy tea or *sake* to drink, nor must their wives.
> Men must plant bamboo or trees round the farmhouse and must use the fallen leaves for fuel so as to save expense.
> Peasants are people without sense or forethought. Therefore they must not give rice to their wives and children at harvest time, but

must save food for the future. They should eat millet, vegetables, and other coarse food instead of rice. Even the fallen leaves of plants should be saved as food against famine. . . . During the season of planting and harvesting, when the labour is arduous, the food taken may be a little better than usual.

The husband must work in the fields, the wife must work at the loom. Both must do night work. However good-looking a wife may be, if she neglects her household duties by drinking tea or sightseeing or rambling on the hill-sides, she must be divorced.

Peasants must wear only cotton or hemp—no silk. They may not smoke tobacco. It is harmful to health, it takes up time, and costs money. It also creates a risk of fire.

The cotton and hemp garments worn by the farmers varied from region to region, and to some extent with the affluence of the wearer, but considerable generalisations can be made. The full-length *kimono* was occasionally worn by both sexes, especially in any moments of relaxation as they had, such as taking part in some local ceremony. The women might wear it in the house during the winter months, when there was little work to do outside, or the men might sometimes wear it at work, tucking its skirts up into their narrow girdle, to give freedom of movement. But work clothes usually consisted of a short jacket worn with a trouser-like garment. In some regions the women wore ample bloomers, drawn in round the ankles, but elsewhere they wore tighter breeches, like their menfolk's but usually with an apron. Both sexes wore girdles about five inches wide. In hot weather men could remove their jackets and work stripped to the waist,

39 Woman's undergarment. A shellfish collector wrings out her underskirt

or go one step further and remove their lower garments, leaving only their loin-cloth, a piece of material passing between the legs and fixed round the hips; it, too, was subject to regional variation in style. The loin-cloth was usually of white cotton, but it could be red, a colour which was believed to keep off demons. Women wore an undergarment rather like a short skirt (*39*), but they did not make any concessions to the warm weather other than to loosen their clothing a little to allow the air to move around their bodies.

Cold-weather wear included leggings, and coverings for the lower arms, the latter with a flap to cover the back of the hands. Straw sandals were the normal footwear, but clogs (*geta*) with high pegs would be worn for walking in mud or a light fall of snow. Districts in the north and east had several feet of snow in the winter, and to cope with such conditions snow-boots of straw, or paddle-shaped snow-shoes or even a primitive sort of ski, were common. Similar paddle-shaped devices were sometimes worn to prevent the wearer from sinking too far into the mud of the rice-fields, although in some fields it was more convenient to move around in punts, even for planting. To keep off the rain or snow the countryman would wear a cloak made of lengths of straw sewn together, with a hood or conical straw hat on his head, the latter also doing duty in the summer. Once again, in the shape and decoration of these articles there would be a considerable variation from locality to locality.

40 Farmhouses with characteristic roof-shapes

The basic food of the farmer and his family, as directed in the ordinance, was not the steamed rice that the *samurai* and rich townsmen enjoyed but a sort of porridge of which millet, or perhaps some barley or wheat, formed the greater part. Green

66

41 Typical hearth. The screen kept draughts off the guest's back. The head of the household sat on the rectangular mat, with his wife (on the round mat) opposite the guest. The roundish block in the foreground is a step at which outside footwear was removed

vegetables, and giant radish pickled in a liquor made from rice-bran accompanied this, along with such fruit as he was unable to sell and the occasional scraping of dried fish to add flavour (and incidentally a little protein to an otherwise largely carbohydrate diet). The rice-fields attracted a lot of wildfowl in the winter months, and some of these may have found their way into the pot, in spite of the Buddhist prohibition against taking life, and fish from the streams were also a delicacy. Beef and horseflesh were never eaten, though the animals' skins were sold when they died. The prohibition on the eating of beef was based on a specific Buddhist principle, probably going back to the sacred cows of India, but it was reinforced by the necessity for keeping cattle for draught purposes, just as horses were required for military use, as pack-animals, and for work on the farm.

The way of life of the farming community was closely linked to the design of the houses: this, too, showed considerable local variation, due partly to climatic influences, and partly to local custom and social organisation, but there were many common features. For example, all houses were of wood-frame construction, with steep roofs and overhanging eaves to allow the heavy rainfall to run off (*40*). The eaves normally projected over a veranda, while the walls of the rooms were often arranged to slide or be removable to allow the free movement of air in the hot, humid summers. The roof was of thatch or faggots, or sometimes of shingles or even tiles. Single-storey houses were most common, but in silk-rearing districts there was very often an upper floor beneath the roof for a silk-room. In some areas of Central Japan, such as parts of the old provinces of Hida and Etchū, the family group was more numerous because it included a wider spread of kinship than elsewhere, and there large houses were the rule, with very steep roofs and three or even four storeys.

One of the consequences of the Japanese preoccupation with cleanliness and the avoidance of pollution was that the ground floor of a house was clearly divided into areas in which the outside footwear could be worn, and those into which one did not go without taking them off. (It was, incidentally, the grossest insult to strike anyone with a sandal or clog.) The beaten-earth floor at an entrance or where rough work was done would be considered an extension of the ground or street outside the house, and stepping up on to the wooden floor of the living-room would mean stepping out of whatever footwear was being worn, and stepping down meant thrusting the feet again into the waiting sandals or *geta*. Very often this earth floor would go right through the house from front to back, with the space on the right taken up with a store, or, in colder regions, there might be a stable instead, open to the rest of the house, so that the horse could be looked after without braving the winter weather, and the animal could share whatever heat there was available with the family. The quarters at the back of the house might be reached along the same earth floor, and could include other stores for tools and equipment, and a scullery with places for washing vegetables, the water being brought into a wooden trough, perhaps by a bamboo pipe from a convenient stream, perhaps carried in buckets. There might also be a stove for cooking the grain that made up the meal, though this was not necessarily in the back. In such a house, to the left of the earthen passageway, was the fireplace, which was truly the focus of life in the house: it provided warmth, and facilities for cooking, and was where the occupants had their meals. In the illustration (*41*) the earthen passage is in the foreground, and the raised planking is the living area, with the fire at one end of a sort of trench. The firing was wood or other inflammable vegetable matter, the smoke from which was considerable, rising upwards to the roof, where it would make its way out, sometimes through holes or gratings at the ends of the topmost ridge.

Status in the family was indicated and rigidly maintained by the seating round the fire. The head of the house, that is, the senior active male, the grandfather of the young children, always had the place facing the passage, and his wife sat (or rather knelt) at right angles to him, in a position facing towards the entrance to the house at the end of the passage. The other fixed seat was opposite to the wife, and was the guest's place, where any honoured guest would sit to have his meal. (If the farmer was an important man, such as the headman of a village, there might be a reception room in the position behind the guest's place, that is, at the front of the house, with a separate entrance, through which a visitor of *samurai* rank might come to do business: such an important guest would not demean himself by sitting at the fire, but would remain in the reception room, and be offered refreshment there, though it was by no means certain that he would deign to partake of it.) If there was no guest, then that place would be occupied by the eldest son or the eldest daughter's husband. The other menfolk, younger sons and farmhands, would sit where they could at the end opposite the head, but the rest of the women, including the eldest son's wife, did the cooking and the fetching and carrying, and ate in snatches in the scullery or after the others had finished, or even, if work pressed, would have to make do with a hasty bowl, sitting on the edge of the planking, remaining in the passageway without removing their footwear.

Around the fire there would be a few pieces of equipment, such as a trivet and some pokers, or a pair of iron bars, held like chopsticks, to serve as tongs; and, most characteristic, the hook suspended over the fire from which hung a kettle or cauldron, adjustable for height and held in position by a jamming-bar, which was often in the shape of a fish: this fish was sometimes thought to be the residence of a household god of fire.

The other rooms in the house would depend for their equipment upon the circumstances of the family. The living-room would normally be boarded, with some straw mats or cushions for the important members of the household to sit on. If the family was above the level of extreme poverty, the wife of its head might have a small room of her own with thick mats as floor covering: this was softer to sit on, and more comfortable to sleep on. There might be survivors of the generation older than the family-head—still probably a strong influence, even though retired from active control of affairs—with a room for themselves; the elder son and his wife and children might also have a room. In a house preserved in the city of Takayama in Hida one such room was more like a large cupboard under the steeply sloping roof. Servants would sleep where they could. There were no beds as known in China or the West; the Japanese slept, and most still do, on mattresses spread on the floor, one per person, for there was no equivalent to a double bed. Young children slept with their mother until they were big enough to have their own mattress. These mattresses, seldom more than an inch or two thick, were stored in a cupboard by day. Instead of pillows, wooden headrests were used, sometimes padded, positioned under the neck. Of course, *samurai* slept in the same way, but with more luxurious bedclothes. In important farmhouses, where there were many servants, they might have dormitories or even separate rooms, like junior *samurai* in castle-towns, arranged in the upper storey of a large gatehouse.

The head of the family was of course supreme, and all the other members deferred to him. His wife might in fact have considerable influence over him, but this would be exercised discreetly and in private. The normal marriage between children of houses of some substance was a result of negotiation involving two go-betweens or sponsors, with the sentiments of the persons directly concerned being only minimally consulted; the advantages of an alliance between the two families was of greater importance. The bride brought with her a dowry and what might be termed the contents of her bottom drawer—bedding and clothing. The wedding was sanctified in a ceremony conducted by the sponsors, in which there was a ritual exchange of cups of *sake*. With people near the line of poverty or even destitution, family advantage was much less of a consideration, and marriages were far more haphazard and likely to depend upon the feelings that the couple had for each other. Some villages had houses for young people where they might live a communal sort of existence, sometimes with a mixing of the sexes, and in these circumstances there was a good deal of pairing and separating; permanent associations might arise from love or from the pregnancy of the girl. It is probable that at this level a marriage was not recognised until a child was on the way. It was also easy to get rid of a wife, especially if she was childless—the husband had only to send her back to her parents' home with her belongings.

A young bride in a more affluent home can hardly have looked forward to going to her new husband's house, apart from the satisfaction of accomplishing her duty. Many of the chores that had been the responsibility of her mother-in-law were now transferred to her. Many mothers-in-law began a life of leisure and of bullying the new arrival, who had often, in addition to the more strenuous tasks that now fell on her, to act as a sort of maid, combing out her mother-in-law's hair, massaging her shoulders when she complained of being tired; she had also, of course, to look after her husband, a duty which would range from providing delicacies for his meals to giving personal attentions such as cleaning out his ears and washing his feet when he came home from working in the mud. The birth of a son relieved her of some part of the heavier work, but one can only presume that she prayed for the day when she, too, could become a mother-in-law in her turn.

Land-holdings were normally handed on to the eldest son, and younger sons were often in a sorry plight, being obliged to work for their brothers, or going off to work for other farmers; one solution for them was to migrate to the expanding towns. When there were no sons, a son-in-law would be brought in for the eldest daughter. Technically what occurred was the adoption into the family of a son. In this sort of marriage, the dominance of the husband over the wife might not be so marked; in fact, the adopted son-in-law was traditionally an unassertive figure.

Just as the household had its status hierarchy, so too the village itself had a clear-cut class distinction. In his great survey of 1582–98, Hideyoshi had registered the holders of land, and when Ieyasu had assumed power, he did nothing to alter the pattern thus recorded. The names of the farmers that appeared on it formed the class of the *honbyakushō*, 'original farmers'; they were often descendants of long lines of landowners, and some of them had chosen to abandon the sword and become full-time farmers. The larger houses in the village belonged to them, and their families would certainly maintain the formal marriage customs. Below them were the small-holders and landless men, living in small houses, or in the houses of their employers; they had very little status, being the dependants of the land-holders, nor did they appear in the tax-registers, or have the right to join in the various corporate groupings in the village organisation. Nevertheless, in a regulated country like Japan, the existence of these men could not go unrecorded, and the means by which this was done was the religious register. When Christianity became illegal, each family had to become the registered parishioners of a Buddhist temple, and each village had to make an annual return of all its inhabitants, including servants and womenfolk, with their religious affiliations, and declare that every person of every grade had been examined and that no persons suspected of Christianity were to be discovered. This return was signed by the priest of the temple concerned and the village officials.

Each person in the village had his place in the web of interconnection that was characteristic of Japanese society. The *honbyakushō* had to form groups of five, with one of them being appointed as spokesman for the rest. The whole group assumed responsibility for the tax of its members, and could also be punished for the shortcomings of any one of the five. They had to sign an annual pledge not to harbour any criminal. The groups were all responsible to the village headman who was in charge of the village office, and had to answer to the official of the domain of his village. The position of headman was very often hereditary, but sometimes the appointment was either by selection of the lord himself, or by the lord's approval of a former headman's nomination, or in some cases by election by heads of families. There were intermediaries between the five-family groups and the headman, who acted as his assistants, and were chosen either by him or by election from the leaders of the groups. There was another village officer known as the 'farmers' representative', who negotiated for them, transmitted instructions to them, and also on occasions seemed to have acted as a sort of constable for the headman. The headman often belonged to an old family of the district, perhaps one which had established the village, and had chosen to give up the sword for the plough. His position between the villagers and the lord's representatives was sometimes not an enviable one: in some villages he became very much a lord's man, and an instrument of oppression, but from time to time a headman would find himself leading a protest, at the risk of his life, and even being executed for his villagers' misdeeds.

The social connections between village people are often described in terms suggesting that they were parent-child relations. Thus a *honbyakushō* would be father to his own children and any adopted children, but also 'father' to his servants and landless labourers who worked for him. He had a semi-filial relationship with the head of his five-family group, and through him with the headman's assistant and the headman himself. He could look for some protection and favour from his 'fathers', but in return he

42 Famine. A farmer has died of starvation. A neighbour points out to a village official and a Buddhist priest (with his rosary) that the dead man's money was of no avail, for there was no food to be bought

had to support them, by carrying out their decisions, and performing appropriate rituals, such as paying respects, accompanied by presents, at the New Year. He had also the normal filial duties towards his real parents, or his adopted ones, and towards those who had acted as go-betweens at his wedding.

The appointment of headman carried with it either an income or exemption from taxation, and in return for this not only had he the heavy responsibility of representing the village, but also had to deal with much paper work. Annual returns, such as the religious register and the pledge of the five-family groups, had to be seen to, with one copy kept in the office and one passed to the officials; then there were papers connected with occasional events, like the passing through the village of a lord on his way to or from Edo, or some court aristocrat on an official visit to a great shrine. For this sort of event he had to arrange for the road to be swept and sanded, and to see that the required amount of porterage was available, that adequate refreshment was offered and so on. Originally the farmers would have provided their own labour for all this, but as time went on the tendency was for the headman to exact money payments from them in lieu of labour and materials, and to employ labour from the pool of under-employed—small-holders, younger sons and other dependants—which existed in most villages; sometimes special contractors were employed. All the time there was need for copying instructions and filing the copies, passing on the originals to the next village, and generally dealing efficiently with bureaucratic demands.

The greatest responsibility of the headman was the collection of taxes. At regular intervals a survey was made of the village land, taking into account the area of the rice-fields, their productivity, the area of land given over to dwellings, the size of the dry fields and crops, the products of the woodlands, any change in usage such as reclamation of waste land, or reversion to waste of former productive land. Samples of crops were taken, and from all this the amount of rice and other taxes to be exacted was decided upon. Usually some 40–60 per cent of the estimated rice-crop was taken, along with money payments to represent other products. The whole attitude of the officials was that the farmers would do their best to defraud them, so that the straw bales had to have a double skin to avoid spillage, for example, and there was a further percentage of rice exacted to make up for any wastage during transportation.

For various reasons, such as insect damage, failure of the rainy season or ruin brought by a typhoon just as the rice was ripening, crops might fail, and the farmers be unable to produce their taxes. In these circumstances a lord with a large domain and consider-able resources would excuse the payment of part or even the whole of the tax, and even, if his stores allowed it, hand out rice to starving farmers (42). But there were some lords who could not do this, and were hard put to it to get together enough rice to feed their retainers. If their farmers had no rice to hand in, they insisted on the payment of the money equivalent, and if the farmers had not the money, they had to borrow it against the security of future crops, at exorbitant rates of interest. Such a lord might find difficulty in feeding his men even in ordinary years, and would exact a money payment early in the season: here again the farmer would have to mortgage his crop to the money-lender, and in severe cases would have to pledge crops not only for the year in question but for the years ahead.

When things got as bad as this, a farmer would naturally think of abandoning his land and moving off to seek employment elsewhere, either in more favourable rural areas or in the

43 Peasant riot. Peasants attack a *samurai* with bamboo staves and spears, and a spade

developing towns. The selling or abandonment of land was strictly forbidden, but obviously took place regardless of the ban. In an effort to prevent abandonment of holdings, it was ordained that a farmer had to obtain a permit from his *shintō* shrine before he could leave his village. If a farmer left his land, or did not work it for some reason, the group or village would have to take it over, and work it to provide revenue. At the same time great efforts were being made by lords to increase their revenues by opening up new fields, either in the valleys or by land reclamation, and they had considerable difficulty in getting occupiers for them. All sorts of devices were used, such as giving new land to those whose present holdings were of poor quality, giving people bonuses of money or *sake* to take up land, or even, it is reported, obliging those who were unmasked as the lovers of married women to cultivate new fields, presumably as a punishment.

Farmers were thus continually being pressed for money, and if they had no good crops to sell, and could not leave their village, they had to seek other ways of raising it. Many were forced to sell their daughters into what amounted to slavery. The brothels and entertainment districts were provided with their women by this means. A father would receive a loan from the proprietor of such an establishment, in return for the use of her services for so many years. At the end of the term she could go back; often, however, the father had to extend the term in order to obtain a further loan. An outsider who was willing to repay the money advanced to the father could buy the girl out to make her his mistress or his bride. Sometimes a husband would use his young wife in this way to provide for himself or his parents. Although there was considerable distress in individual cases, there was no general condemnation of this practice, because it was seen as one way of serving one's parents, and in the atmosphere of the times it is probable that the majority of girls found their new life at least no worse than the one they were leaving. Should a girl manage to return home eventually she could well be in demand as a wife because of the education and experience of the world which she had acquired while she was away.

Sons, too, would try to relieve the situation at home by taking temporary jobs in a castle-town, and staying on after their contract was terminated, or even by running away to Edo or Osaka, so that they were no longer dependent on their family. The depopulation of the countryside had reached such proportions in the early nineteenth century that the central government carried out forcible repatriations of refugees from rural areas.

Another way of reducing the number of mouths to be fed was the widespread use of infanticide and abortion. In country districts it seems that the former was more common, perhaps because the sex of the child could be determined, babies, especially girls, being smothered at birth. Attempts were made in various domains to control this 'thinning out', as it was called, by demanding that pregnancies be reported and their course inspected, and by giving bounties payable on the birth of a child, but by and large the control was not effective.

From time to time circumstances would drive villagers to attempt recourse to communal action in an effort to ameliorate their situation. Any sort of combination was, of course, illegal, but they protested all the same. Sometimes they tried to complain about the behaviour of a village official, or to get the tax-rate reduced: in one case, which is recorded, word was passed secretly round, and a meeting was held by night on a river-bank (the one available open space), at which members of various villages agreed to make a direct approach to the lord—in itself an illegal procedure, since it ignored the proper channels. Unfortunately for them, spies of the headman of one of the villages were present, and reported the assembly to him. The villagers had to send a letter through the headman to two *samurai* making very fulsome apologies for their wicked action, with reiterated promises not to do such a thing again, and asking them to intercede with their lord. In some other cases, if it was thought that the normal procedure of approaching the headman would be ineffective, there was an attempt to send on a complaint or request by means of a round robin, in which the names of all the villagers, with their seals, were arranged in a circle, so that the identity of the ringleaders should not be disclosed.

When peaceable protest failed, and things were desperate, the villagers joined in an armed rising, although the weapons at their disposal were not normally anything but agricultural tools. It is estimated that some 1,500 peasant revolts (*43*) occurred during this period, ranging from those involving the inhabitants of a single village to one in which those from more than 200 took part. This represents an average of more than six incidents a year, so that while they were hardly a feature of most farmers' lives, news of these risings must have reached everyone's ears, and the thought of them must have been in all minds. One of their characteristics, as it was of all protest in the Tokugawa period, is that they did not seek to overthrow the régime or threaten a local lord, but had only limited objectives and looked for redressment of a specific wrong, such as oppression by certain officials or the insistence on tax-payment in a year of crop failure. A villager seemed to think that it was worth while taking part in a rising provided that somebody else organised it: his participation increased the numbers, making the mob more formidable in appearance, and giving him the opportunity to vent his resentment by smashing down a few doors or burning a house or two in a castle-town, and possibly getting at a rice-store or breaking open some barrels of *sake*. There was a very good chance that the demands would be met. The disturbances themselves seem to have been remarkably bloodless, with the *samurai* making sure of getting out of the way, and being strangely unwilling to open fire on the mob from the castle.

Punishment for the leaders of these risings was, however, often severe. For example, at one place in North Japan, the crops had failed in 1745 and 1746 and by early 1747 there was no more rice available. The local authorities refused to permit rice to be brought in from outside, and 33 villages rose and presented a series of demands, largely concerning local conditions. These were granted, and in addition the farmers received a considerable sum of money and an issue of rice. But then the reprisals began. The leaders were arrested, and confessed under torture. Eventually, five leaders were executed, and some of their relatives sent into exile. Seventeen farmers and four group-leaders received heavy fines, but it is clear that the majority of those who took part in the rising reaped only the benefits. In folk memory and in plays there is often the suggestion that the leaders of such a rising went into it with the full knowledge that death might well be the outcome for them, but they considered that the benefit to the community made their sacrifice worth while. The high proportion of cases in which the leaders were punished would lend colour to this interpretation.

In most of the literature of the time the farmer is depicted as a crude, uncultured creature, with little in his favour. It must be realised, however, that this was largely written for townspeople, who fancied themselves as smart and progressive, enjoying themselves as only they knew how, and despising anything rustic. The *samurai* thought of the farmers most often as near-criminals, out to deprive them of their just dues. The farmer clearly did his best to keep to a minimum the amount of rice and tax that he handed over, and there is no doubt that surveyors were bribed or deceived whenever possible into not recording new fields, or that domain administration was sometimes slack enough not to carry out surveys, so that the percentage of tax actually handed over was less than the full amount due. The sentiment expressed by some warriors that the farmers always had good rice to eat might have been true from time to time and from place to place, but the frequency of the risings, and the practices, against human nature, of infanticide and child-selling, must indicate that life for many must have been very hard.

In every village, however, there were times in the year when people enjoyed themselves. The New Year was the time for the farmer to visit his patrons, and for his dependants to visit him: at this season small pine trees were brought down from the mountains and placed at the gate, and round rice-cakes, made from especially glutinous rice, were offered to the various gods who watched over the home—looking after the fire or the kitchen—and to the spirits of the ancestors inscribed in the household Buddhist altar, and were, needless to say, eaten in large quantities by children and

78

adults. All sorts of ritual, loosely thought of as *shintō*, took 'place, and there was hardly a village but did not have something exciting to look forward to—even in the north, with its snowy winter, strange wild men might appear and burst into houses and frighten the children until appeased with refreshment. At the village *shintō* shrine, which was often the residence of the god or ancestral spirit of the oldest family, there was usually some fertility or hunting dance, or some representation of myth, interspersed with comically obscene dances, performed by young men of certain restricted families, and this was an occasion when the whole village would turn out to watch. Perhaps the most widespread festivity of all was that of the midsummer *bon* dances in

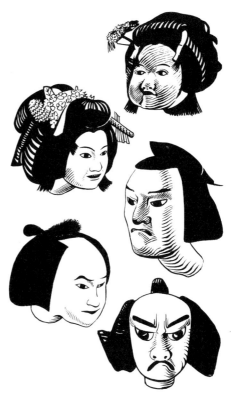

44 Heads of puppets dating from the nineteenth century. The male head at the bottom has moving eyes and eyebrows

July, which were Buddhist. At that time the souls of the dead were thought to return to earth, and the villagers would dance for their entertainment. These *bon* dances, and the songs that go with them, have survived until today, although many have become separated from their local origins, and form one section of the repertory of traditional performers all over Japan. They are processional or circular dances, by men and women together, with a group of older persons providing the accompaniment, typically a combination of drums, flutes and *shamisen* (a three-stringed instrument played with the hand or plectrum). In some regions the dances are very energetic, but more often

79

山
伏

45 *Yamabushi*. An adept of the mountain cult, blowing his conch. The pillbox-hat, the bobbles at the front, the design on the breeches, and the staff, all had a mystic significance

they are slow and graceful, with languorous hand and arm movements, in keeping with the sultry heat of the season. The words of the songs are more often than not in praise of the region. As the sun set, the heat and the excitement of the day had their effect, along with the *sake* that was drunk, and orgiastic scenes are said to have developed. The *bon* festivals brought with them a great release from tension, and in a society the members of which were incessantly concerned with their obligations and their status, such a relaxation of normal standards was of the greatest psychological benefit.

Other opportunities for enjoyment were rare but not entirely absent. Weddings were celebrated with wine and food for all, with the bride having to do a great deal of the entertaining: no honeymoon privacy for her, and as the whole emphasis was on her duty to her husband and his family, she did not really expect to get any pleasure out of a marriage, so she was not disappointed—the status and security were sufficient compensation. Other excuses for a good time involved communal labour, such as rice-planting, well-digging, and re-roofing, and, of course, a successful harvest had to be rounded off with as great a feast as could be afforded.

Agricultural festivities came round every year, but the supreme opportunity for enjoyment for the poorer farmers came only once in a lifetime, with the pilgrimage to Ise. The great shrine of Ise, on the east of the Kii peninsula, and reached by a diversion from the great road between Edo and Osaka, had been established in early times as the shrine of the sun goddess, the ancestress of the Imperial family. It was not until the sixteenth century that commoners had gone to worship there, but during the Tokugawa period the number of pilgrims increased greatly, and it became the ambition of nearly everyone in Japan to go there at least once in a lifetime. The actual act of worship was not complicated; it consisted of going to each of the two shrines that made up the Ise complex, prostrating before the sanctuary, clapping one's hands to call the attention of the goddess, and, in return for a contribution to the shrine funds, receiving protective tablets and amulets to take back home. There were other small shrines and also temples to be visited, but by the seventeenth century the main object of the trip for the pilgrim was the entertainment that was available when he got there.

At Ise there was a street called Furuichi, full of brothels, eating-houses and souvenir shops, and there was also the chance of seeing a *kabuki* play, or the puppets (*44*), or less artistic performances—juggling, conjuring, freaks and so on—at the theatres that were set up in the enclosures of the temples and shrines, but not of the great shrine itself, which maintained an ambience of sanctity. Ise had the most important theatre group outside the main centres of Edo, Kyoto and Osaka, and was also a stopping-place on the circuit that actors from these centres followed during the summer months, between rice-planting and the harvest, when the farmers could take time off from the fields more easily. Only the richer farmers could afford to go at their own expense, and although men were in the majority, women could go too; it could be one of the things a woman looked forward to being able to do when her son got married and his wife took over the hard work.

The poorer farmers, however, were not deprived of the opportunity of going to Ise, for there was a widespread custom of forming Ise-associations, the members of which contributed a certain amount to the general fund, and sufficient was accumulated each year to send a certain number of members. The order in which they went was determined by lot, and the lucky ones were accompanied to the village boundaries by the entire populace. They were thought of as representatives of the whole community, and brought back enough amulets for distribution to all. The priests of Ise had agents throughout the country who made the necessary arrangements both for the journey (on foot, of course), and for the actual time spent in the vicinity of the shrine. For such people the pilgrimage to Ise might very well be the only chance to see the outside world, with its wonders and its opportunity for pleasure.

Ise was the most important shrine to be visited on a national scale, but there were others, like Miyajima in the west of Japan, and Kotohira in Shikoku, which had a more local appeal. Other religious trips that farmers might take part in were connected with the very widespread mountain cult, which combined climbing mountains, such as Fuji, or peaks in Yoshino, with feats of endurance, exemplified by standing under waterfalls (45). Although the religious content of these pursuits was high, considerable importance was also attached to the festivities that concluded the rites.

By the beginning of the nineteenth century, the rural communities had, if one ignores the bad years of famine, a higher standard of living than before, and one result of this, and the improvement of communications that accompanied it, was the spread of the drama to villages. We begin to read accounts of visits by professional actors to rural areas, including typical contemptuous townsmen's stories of country audiences, of the stupidity of extras recruited locally, and even anecdotes that can surely be matched all over the world of the ill-behaviour on the stage of a horse that the company had to use, because of shortage of manpower, to replace the more predictable *kabuki* animal played by two actors. From this period date the majority of the village stages that are known from the region of the Inland Sea and from the mountainous areas behind Edo. They are usually built in the precincts of the village shrine, and consist of a covered stage, complete with traps and revolving stage, worked by manpower from the dressing room below, known as the 'underworld'. Technically, performances on them were given to amuse the god of the shrine, but the audience, sitting in the open for a performance lasting several hours, eating, drinking, laughing, crying, feeding their babies, slipping back home to relieve themselves so as not to waste precious fertiliser, obviously took their share of the pleasure. Performances might be of live actors or puppets, and were sometimes given by strolling players, sometimes by local amateur talent. If the former, the local inhabitants had to be careful not to allow them to stay in their homes for fear of official rebuke, but they could usually be found accommodation in the temple precincts. The strolling puppeteers, often from the island of Awaji, but also from Awa or Kyūshū (the base of some wandering *kabuki* actors as well), were beneath the class system, but tradition has it that the lords of domains used them as convenient sources of intelligence about what was going on in the neighbours' lands. Some villages acquired sets of puppets and put on their own shows, using playbooks and descriptions brought back by villagers who had gone on pilgrimage.

In the early years of the Tokugawa period, farmers had usually not been allowed to see plays because the authorities feared that the sight of luxurious living would make them want to improve their standards, and also that time might thus be wasted, reducing their rice-production. The growth of the rural drama was therefore symptomatic of the fact that the grip of the warrior class on the country was slackening.

4

The Craftsmen

The third and fourth of the four classes of Tokugawa society are the craftsmen and the merchants. In the larger towns, at least, they became closely intermingled, and often it would be difficult to say of any one person to which class he belonged. In this and the next chapter will be found an account of their professional life; the last chapter of this book will deal in general with life in the great towns, how the inhabitants spent their leisure, and what other members of the family would be doing while the head of the family was earning its living.

When the craftsmen were put into third place below farmers but above merchants, Hideyoshi or his advisers were probably thinking of them as suppliers of articles to the warriors in the castle-towns—either necessary equipment or things with an artistic or decorative function. It would have been of no interest to them that the same craftsmen might provide similar articles to rich commoners and certainly any such work would have to be put aside if an order came in from the castle. Figures are available for the town of Tsuyama, the seat of a *daimyō* who was an outside lord of Mimasaka province, a medium-sized domain, in the mountains inland from Okayama. In 1665 there were in this town nearly 1,000 houses occupied by warriors of all ranks, including foot-soldiers, with about 4,000 other houses in which lived townsfolk of all sorts. There is a list of the craftsmen in the town: they include three blacksmiths, eight sword-sharpeners, four silver-smiths, three scabbard-workers, two lacquerers, two shaft-makers, and one worker in cypress wood. All these were specialists in the manufacture of equipment for the warriors, but there were other craftsmen more generally employed. There was only one dyer, but no less than 98 *sake*-brewers, as well as 222 carpenters, 37 sawyers,

84

six plasterers (*46*), and an un-
specified number of coopers,
shinglers, thatchers, paperers,
tobacco-cutters, tilers and mat-
makers (*47*).

The blacksmiths were almost
certainly sword-makers (*48*).
Their craft was a highly skilled
one, conducted in a semi-
religious atmosphere, with the
workshop surrounded by a
boundary-rope as if it were a
shintō shrine. Sword-sharpeners
did the general servicing of
sword-blades (which needed
considerable attention, being
very prone to rust), and put on
them the razor-sharp edge which
made them so formidable. The
shaft-makers were concerned
with the handles of spears and
halberds.

46 A plasterer and his mate.
The drawing is taken from a
collection of 100 views of Fuji
by Hokusai. The scaffolding is
clearly depicted

Many of the other craftsmen
were occupied with the building
of houses, and of these the car-
penters stood out, being responsible for the erecting of buildings,
seeing to the timber framework for the walls and roof, and controlling the work of the other tradesmen. As for the walls, these
were made by the plasterers of mud-mortar with a mixture of straw.
Paperers were employed for covering the light lattice-work of the
sliding screens, which had to be translucent while preventing
draughts and prying glances. Mat-makers produced the thick
straw mats, covered with a special grass, that were laid over the
plank floors in the houses of the well-to-do.

The Japanese, who love to classify, divide the craftsmen into
those to whom the customer comes (that is, those who have a
workshop in which to ply their trade), and those, like carpenters,
who have to go to the place where the work is to be done. There
was a third category, the wandering or itinerant craftsmen—and
these can again be subdivided into those whose trade made them

47 Two mat-makers. The one on the right is busy with the straw that makes up the bulk of the mat, the other is resting from his labour of covering this with the special grass used for the purpose. This covering would, in time, wear out, but could be replaced

wanderers, and those who pursued a calling that could be done from a temporary base. Among the former were certain wood-workers, who, like woodturners in the beech woods of England, would travel with their portable lathes making household utensils. These people led a completely nomadic existence, and managed to avoid official registration until after the end of the Tokugawa period. Another such group were the tappers of lac (*49*). They obtained from the lacquer tree, which was mainly to be found in the northern parts of Japan, the raw material which the lacquer-workers applied to a basis of wood or other substance to make utensils, furniture or other objects. Lac might be called a natural varnish, which gives a surface of great beauty, and which, being a good insulator, keeps liquids hot when they are served in it. The raw lac is extracted in spring and summer, by means of horizontal channels cut in the trunk of the tree; it exudes into these channels, and is removed by a sort of scraper. It was collected in buckets and transported in air-proof tubs. The tappers worked for the owners of the trees, and surrounded their craft with an atmosphere of secrecy typical of an age when admission to a trade was comparable to a privileged initiation into a secret society.

Yet another group of travellers were the *sake*-brewers (*50*). The great centres for the producing of *sake* were near the coast of the Inland Sea to the west of Osaka, in towns like Ikeda, Itami and Nishinomiya. The process is fundamentally a breaking down of rice-grains by a fungus, and the production by fermentation of an alcoholic liquid, *sake*, which was drunk at all sorts of celebrations and festivities. It was warmed before being served, when it was poured into very small cups. Its manufacture was limited to the winter season, and provided a very convenient off-season employment for men from the northern parts. *Sake*-brewing for home consumption was also a winter occupation on larger farms, and well-to-do town families would also employ specialists to come and make *sake* on the premises, from rice that they had bought for the purpose.

The other category of wandering craftsmen did the same sort of things as their town counterparts, but travelled from village to village. Farming communities were, of course, capable of doing

48 Two sword-smiths forge a blade. They wear ceremonial dress, and an untrimmed straw-rope with paper streamers, as used to bound sacred enclosures, testifies to the semi-religious atmosphere

many things for themselves: they could certainly build simple houses and do ordinary carpentry, while roof-renewal was the occasion for a communal effort followed by some merrymaking. But more decorative or elegant work would have to wait until a skilled man came round or was summoned. In the early part of the period, such a man, apart from being respected for his skill, was welcome as a bringer of news from the outside world, and sometimes he would settle down to a pampered spell of idleness, fed by the villagers for the entertainment he gave them, and having, it is reported, the pick of the village girls. Later on, with the improvements in communications and the development of distributing enterprises, merchants could bring the products of craftsmanship to villages, and the wandering expert fell on hard times.

All craftsmen, however, whether they operated from the fixed workshop or wandered abroad, worked with their hands, with occasional help from their feet and legs, or their mouth, on natural materials. They had only a few machines such as the wood-worker's lathe, the potter's wheel, the smith's bellows, the spinner's wheel, the weaver's loom, and the rice-pounder for removing husks. Their tools were planes, saws, chisels, knives and

49 Lac-tappers at work

shears, all of very fine quality, for the swordsmith's superb forging of steel was only the apex of a whole tradition of skilful manufacture in this metal. All the delicate techniques had to be instilled into hand and eye from an early age. The apprentice, who might be the younger son of some other townsman, or a country boy from a large family, would live in his master's home, and be under a filial obligation to him. The real son of the household would also learn his father's trade, but his hope would be to take over the workshop

50 *Sake*-brewing

when his father retired. The apprentice expected to be able to set up on his own. His training period was normally seven or eight years, and at the end of that time he was expected to work out of gratitude to his master for a further six or 12 months. After this, he might be given a share of his master's *clientèle* as a foundation for his own business, or have his status as an independent workman recognised by employers. Alternatively, he might stay on at his master's as a journeyman. His training was not only in the actual techniques required in his craft, but also in what might be called its lore and its vocabulary, the latter amounting to a secret language in which the craftsman could communicate, partly with the object of concealing their hard-won knowledge from the public at large, and partly as a code whereby one trained man might recognise another.

In the 1660s a craftsman more often than not ran an independent business, working to orders from his clients and occupying what time he had to spare in making articles for stock, against a possible purchaser. It was very seldom that he made a fortune, or even amassed any capital to enable him to develop his business.

51 Stone-masons carving a lantern, and *koma-inu*, statues of dogs which guard the entrance of *shintō* shrines

In the castle-towns, prices were strictly controlled — swords were paid for according to length, not for their quality or their decoration—and, in any case, by all accounts, debts were not easy to collect when warriors owed them. Money payments could be only part of the reward for labour. The wandering craftsman who set up his workshop in a village would have most of the materials provided for him from local resources, and the board and lodging he received would go a long way towards paying for his work.

Perhaps the most affluent craftsmen were those who worked for the Shogun and the *daimyō*, and those connected with the building trade, the 'five crafts' of the carpenter, plasterer, stonemason (*51*), sawyer and roofer. The sawyer cut the timbers the carpenter needed, the plasterer covered the solid walls, the roofer used thatch, shingles or tiles, the stonemason was concerned with the platform on which the building stood, or the stones on which pillars were erected, and also with stone lanterns and basins and burial monuments. The carpenter was in charge of the whole building operation, and performed the same sort of function as the building contractor in Britain: his services were in constant demand in towns (where population tended always to increase), even when there were no natural disasters, but especially after a fire or earthquake, when wide areas had to be reconstructed. Such disasters afforded opportunities for young craftsmen just out of apprenticeship; they had only to demonstrate their skill to be taken on at a good wage. Fortunes were sometimes founded at these times of crisis by selling a local supply of wood at highly inflated prices, or by cornering the market.

Among Ihara Saikaku's descriptions (see p. 63) there is one of Edo carpenters and roofers coming home after a day's work in *daimyō* mansions:

They were in their groups, 200–300 at a time, and were chattering in high discordant tones. Their side-locks stood out from their cheeks, and their hair was in disorder. Their clothes were dirty at the collar, and they wore their belts over their jackets, which were torn at the cuffs. Some used their rules as walking-sticks, most hunched their shoulders, with their hands thrust into the front of their *kimono*, and from their back view as they walked along there was no need of a sign to show what trade they were. Behind them came their mates and apprentices, who were carrying the shavings and cut-off ends, but no one cared if some precious cypress end-bits fell and were left behind.

The roofers have especially shrill voices to enable them to shout at each other when on the job, and they wear their belts outside their jackets instead of beneath them to stop them getting caught up when they are climbing about. The characteristic economy of materials is shown in the apprentices' task of taking back the shavings and unused ends of wood, contrasting with the carefree attitude of not picking up any that might fall. The story goes on to tell how a poor man gathered this wood and sold it, or made chopsticks from it and sold them, and finished up as a prosperous timber merchant.

The exuberant characters described in this passage had the double advantage of being both builders and in the employ of *daimyō*. They probably received their pay in the form of a rice-allowance, as did all the 'appointed' craftsmen. Some of these who were attached to the Shogun or rich lords were the prominent artists of the period, such as the painters of the Kano and Tosa families; included in their number were the lacquerers and wood-carvers, and in fact members of all the crafts. These 'appointed' craftsmen were sometimes honoured by being given *samurai* privileges: a commoner was not normally entitled to the use of a surname, but many outstanding craftsmen were allowed this sign of status, and some were also given the right to wear two swords. All were permitted to sign their work, as, in fact, were carpenters, who could put their name on the houses they built: this was forbidden to ordinary craftsmen.

The attitude to craft was very like that of the medieval counterparts in Europe, with their system of training and its culmination in initiation into the society of men with the same skill. This comparison must not be carried too far—in particular the participation of craftsmen in municipal government was far more advanced in Europe than in Japan—but there are further points of resemblance. Men in the same craft lived together in the same quarter of the town, just as street-names in old cities in Europe indicate what they did there; in Japan the authorities are said to have encouraged if not required this grouping, to facilitate control. The craftsmen in a town also had their associations—one might almost use the word 'guild'—to supervise their standards and act as benevolent societies. Some of these associations had protective deities in the *shintō* pantheon, like patron saints in Europe: that of the blacksmiths was Inari, the rice god whose messenger is a fox, and this relationship is demonstrated in a *nō* play, which shows the god helping the swordsmith with a particularly difficult job. There was usually an annual meeting or festival, and this helped to maintain the solidarity of the group. The more affluent members, in particular those with connections with the great households, were the leaders, often called 'the elders', and spokesmen of these associations, in which the lowly craftsmen took but a humble role. In a work dated 1774 craftsmen are enjoined to concentrate upon their craft.

> You should have engraved upon your heart the realisation that there is no way of earning more than enough for each to live on. No matter how poor you are, you must not be beguiled into another trade. If you ply your craft unchangingly and with complete devotion, the time may come when you will prosper.

They are advised to work cheerfully, to maintain honesty and exactitude, not to envy those in other crafts, not to refuse any commissions even though the price of materials has risen and profit could thereby grow less, and to live contented with their lot.

Many followed these injunctions, either through necessity or virtue, but some were more concerned with financial gain, and, by employing the cheap labour of many apprentices, expanded their sales. In any case, the actual status of craftsmen underwent a change as the period went on; from working for individual clients, they became more and more workmen employed by capitalists. These were owners of warehouses who became middle-men between the craftsman and his customer, and who tended to debase the old values by thinking more of price and quantity than of quality, and who did not hesitate to bring in untrained labour. Some of this came from the ranks of the warriors, the poorest of

52 Lacquer chest—the front of a superb example in the Victoria and
Albert Museum in London

whom had to take on hand work to eke out their rice-incomes;
they seemed to turn to umbrella- and clog-making for preference,
and of course often did clerical work. Those who fell into the
power of warehouse-owners were generally workers who made
things for sale rather than craftsmen such as builders and others
who provided services, and who maintained a greater degree of
independence.

The authorities exacted their tribute from the craftsmen as from
the other classes. Property-owners in towns paid a form of tax, but
the majority of craftsmen rented their houses. They made their
contribution in the form of goods or services, in much the same
way as the farmer and his forced labour, and a money payment
was often substituted. Inventors of some devices and processes also
made a payment in order to acquire something like patent rights.

Many of the methods used by craftsmen in their various trades
were very similar to those used in the West, once certain differences
are allowed for: the Japanese was used to sitting on the floor, and
this brought his feet and hands nearer together than when working
at a bench or sitting on a stool, so that in the West feet could work
treadles for lathes or potter's wheels, while in Japan they could be

used for applying pressure to hold something still while work was done on it. Differences of detail also arose from the fact that the saw and the plane worked on the pulling rather than the pushing stroke. A line wetted with ink served the same purpose as the British workman's chalk-line (*53*).

One material available to the Japanese craftsman that Europe did not know was lacquer. Apart from the utensils already mentioned, lacquer is also the basis of decorative patterns used to embellish all sorts of furniture—reading-desks, tables, writing-cabinets, toilet-boxes, dressing-tables—and equipment such as armour and palanquins. It occupied the place which was taken in Europe by inlaying, painting and varnishing (*52*). Another material that had countless uses of wide utility was bamboo: cut and trimmed, it made fences, poles and masts; with its nodal divisions bored through it made pipes for leading water down a hill-side, the natural taper making it easy to join lengths by pushing the narrow end of one into the wider end of the next. Bamboo can be split into neat sections and slivers and used for basketry, lattices and screens, as well as for receptacles such as cups and ladles. In conjunction with paper (that also had wide application from paper handkerchiefs to clothing), it was used for making both flat and folding fans, some headgear, and the frames of umbrellas (to be covered with oiled paper) and of paper lanterns. Paper was made from the fibres of the inner bark of trees, especially the mulberry, but not from rags, and its production formed a considerable industry, with regional specialities, and a very wide variety of products. For example, even in the tenth century the colour and pattern of the paper a poem was written on had an importance nearly as great as the quality of the poem itself, and in the Tokugawa period, when it came to writing letters, the paper used had to have the appropriate quality and thickness. Book-production was considerable, while paper required for the home had to be frequently renewed, and thus demand was constant.

Printing was normally from wooden blocks, one block to a page, carved from a hand-written original; coloured prints had one block for each colour. Printing was by hand, using only brushes and pads, with no machinery for inking. Writing was done with a brush, of which there were many sizes according to the size of the writing to be done; they are made of animal hair set into a bamboo tube. The ink is compounded from lamp-black and

53 Carpenters and their tools—planes, saws, chisels, adze, mallet, whetstone and ink-line

glue, kneaded and worked into sticks. These are used with an ink-stone, of fine-grained slate or the like, which has a flat surface with a sunken end into which water is put. Some of the water is transferred to the flat part by dipping the ink-block in it, and the ink for writing is produced by rubbing the block and water on the stone, from which it is taken by the brush. The making of high-quality ink and stone took a great deal of skill and experience.

The weaving of cloth was widespread in country districts as an occupation for the womenfolk on a farm, and a large proportion of the hemp- and cotton-weaving, and the plainer sort of silk-weaving, was done in this way. The material was produced in standard rolls, measuring about two feet by 20 yards, each of which was enough to make one *kimono*. The process of making up the material required a certain amount of skill, to accommodate it approximately to the size of the wearer, but in view of the fact that the garment has no buttons or other fastening, but is held together by the girdle, while the woman's *kimono* is adjusted by a larger or smaller tuck under the wide girdle, the services of a professional dressmaker were not needed by a normal household, especially as the stitching is not the fine stitching of the West, but is more like tacking. Washing a *kimono* involved taking it to pieces, washing and starching them separately, on frames, and reassembling, changing round the pieces to distribute wear.

Silk cloth was often highly decorative. It could have various textures and damask effects, and also patterns derived from the use of differently coloured thread, worked in at the time of weaving. It could have patterns dyed in after weaving, either by a process similar to painting, whereby colours were brushed on to the fabric, or by knot-dyeing, in which small areas of the cloth were drawn up into bunches before the whole was immersed in the dye; when the bunches were undone, there was left a small area in the original colour. Finally, designs could be embroidered on the fabric to produce a brocade.

Whereas various regions of Japan could produce patterned weaving, complicated dyeing and embroidery was done in towns, the most celebrated area being Nishijin, a district in the north-west of Kyoto, with a long history of work for the court, and later for the Shogun.

The isolation of Japan until the middle of the nineteenth century preserved, until a period when Europe and America were well into the era of mass production, a tradition of handicraft which Europe had known some centuries earlier but had now nearly forgotten. While in their own specialities the best craftsmen were probably not inferior to those of Japan, it can be claimed that the demand by the warrior class for articles which their cult of simplicity required should be elegant and tasteful, coupled with the size of this demand (which may well have been greater than that of the aristocratic patrons of the West), meant that craft products in Japan were on the whole superior to their Western counterparts.

5

The Merchants

In the previous chapter it was pointed out how many tradesmen, from being largely independent, producing their goods to order and selling them in their own workshops, became mere paid workers for merchant-houses. Throughout the Tokugawa period merchants were disliked and increasingly feared by the authorities. Originally the merchant was put at the bottom of the class system because he was considered a parasite, adding nothing to the economy: it was merely by the handling of goods and produce that were the fruit of another's toil that he received money and so made his livelihood. Nevertheless, the merchant class rose to a position of ever greater influence and power as time went on, symptomatic of the change from a feudal to a commercial society. As the merchants flourished, so many *samurai* became increasingly impoverished, and as both lived in towns, the monied traders exerted more and more influence on the *samurai*, partly through intermarriage and partly through a more materialistic view of life, some *samurai* even selling their status for money.

A useful introduction to an account of how the merchants operated will be a description of the coinage (*55*), which was fairly intricate, since it involved the use of four metals, gold, silver, copper and iron. Complications arose from time to time following efforts by the central government to improve the economy by debasing or improving the content of the coinage, which was not even uniform over the whole country, gold forming the currency in Edo, while Osaka and Kyoto used silver. Copper, however, was everywhere in use, although it was sometimes replaced by iron or brass.

Starting from the unit of lowest value, the *zeni* was a circular copper coin about one inch in diameter with a quarter-inch square hole in the centre. These were first made in Japan in 1636; up to then coins minted in China or even in Korea or Annam had been current. One *zeni* could buy such things as a cup of tea or a rest at a wayside stall (*54*); but very often they were strung together with a strand of hemp through the central holes to make a 'string of cash'. These were of two sizes, one with a nominal 100 coins, and the other with a nominal 1,000. These figures had been the actual number before 1636, but since 96 of the new Japanese coins had been declared equivalent to 100 of the old Chinese ones, the custom arose in most districts of having strings of 96 and 960 respectively. The 1,000 string was equivalent in value to a rectangular gold coin, 0·7 by 0·4 inch, known as *ichibu kin*, i.e. one *bu* of gold, *bu* being a weight used in weighing gold. Four *bu* of gold equalled one *ryō* (just over 18 grammes), which was the weight of the most common gold coin, known as the *koban*. This was a thin plate of gold, more or less elliptical in shape, 2·8 by 1·5 inches.

There was also a larger gold coin still, the *ōban*, theoretically weighing ten *ryō*, but actually between eight and nine. It was not, however, in common commercial use, being reserved for ceremonial purposes. At various times smaller gold coins were produced, and these were the only ones in this metal that the ordinary family would be likely to have in its possession. *Koban* were used only for transactions involving members of the warrior class, or fairly large merchant-houses.

Kyoto and Osaka used silver as the superior metal to copper.

54 Wayside teashop: the sign outside reads 'Food for one *zeni*'. The customers include a Buddhist priest. The waitress on the left is carrying a flask of *sake*. The travellers wear straw sandals, the waitresses wooden clogs (*geta*)

Coins were of various shapes and sizes, the largest being the *chōgin*, an elliptical coin, often quite roughly finished, measuring about 3·6 by 1·2 inches. The unit of silver weight was the *monme*, and this piece weighed about 43 *monme* (a little over 161 grammes). A smaller coin, the *mame-ita*, was hardly more than a rounded lump of silver,

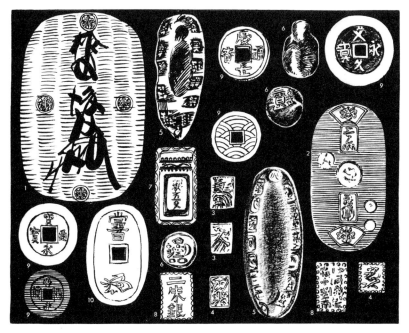

55 Coins. Gold: (1) ōban (2) koban (3) ichibu kin (4) other denominations. Silver: (5) chōgin (6) mame-ita (7) 5 monme piece (8) other denominations. Copper: (9) zeni (10) unusual 100 zeni coin

of indefinite weight and dimensions, with a mark stamped on it to testify to the quality of the metal. At various times there appeared smaller denominations, rectangular in shape and of fixed weight.

For large sums, silver coinage was made up into packets of convenient weight, such as 100 monme and 500 monme, while gold koban were made into neat packs of 25, 50 or 100, covered with strong paper and stamped either with a government seal or that of a large concern. The normal practice was to use these packs without opening them. For transporting and storing larger sums, special wooden strong-boxes were made to hold a fixed amount: 1,000-ryō boxes were in most common use.

The ordinary person carried his zeni in a draw-purse which he kept in the bosom of his kimono, where it was safe and prevented from falling out by the girdle. Small pieces of silver were carried in the same way, but small amounts of gold were stowed in flat cases very similar to the wallets used in the West for banknotes.

Paper money was in fact not used by the central authorities in Tokugawa Japan except in the last year of its existence, but it was issued in some of the domains. Early in the Tokugawa period, when the assumption of the sole right of coinage by the Edo government, and the drain of species to foreign countries through Nagasaki, left the provinces short of coins, notes expressed in gold, silver or copper values were printed and used by the *daimyō* to fulfil their obligations. Between 1701 and 1730 they were prohibited, but were in restricted use again after that date.

In 1701 there occurred the famous incident when the lord of the Akō domain in Harima was provoked by an insult into drawing his sword in the Edo Palace. For this he was condemned to take his life, his estates being confiscated. After his death 47 of his retainers (now *rōnin*) formed an association to avenge his death. How they did this, and their consequent suicide, is the subject of many plays and stories about the 'Loyal League'. As soon as the sentence on their master was passed, one of them went from Edo to the home castle, and covered the 400 miles in a palanquin in five days; an ordinary traveller would have taken at least 17 days, and even an express messenger would have needed eight. The relevant point of this story is that, when Ōishi, the senior retainer, heard of his master's fate, his first thought was for the holders of notes issued by the domain. He counted the gold in the treasury and found that it represented some 60 per cent of the note issue so he had the paper money exchanged at this rate, thus enabling the holders of the notes to rescue something from the wreck, and incidentally depriving the Shogun of a sizeable sum. Those who got their money were lucky, for although convertibility was a condition of permission for an issue, these local notes showed at some time or other the usual vicissitudes of convertibility and non-convertibility, devaluation and inflation.

The mutual exchange values of the coins made from the various metals were in a constant state of change throughout the period, in spite of efforts by the authorities to stabilise them. At the beginning, in 1609, the exchange rate was one *ryō* of gold to 50 *monme* of silver to four strings of *zeni*, but soon after silver declined to 60 *monme*. The gold to silver ratio remained more or less at this level until the middle of the nineteenth century, when the influence of world exchange rates brought down the price of silver until one *ryō* equalled a hundred *monme*. Copper, too, tended to decline in

56 Money-changer's. The clerks are busy weighing (using balance and steelyard), calculating on the *soroban*, counting and transporting strings of cash. Customers enjoy a pipe while waiting. A *samurai* and a woman pass by

relation to gold. In the last quarter of the eighteenth century it slipped to six strings to one *ryō*, and in the 1860s it went to ten strings. These broad changes were accompanied by short-term and local fluctuations which could be used by the money-changers as a source of speculative profits.

With three different coinage metals current in the country, it was very necessary to have a means of swiftly changing from one to the other. Most retail trade was transacted in copper, and large shopkeepers and wholesalers needed to change this into gold or silver for settling their debts, and the reverse operation was required, for example, when a merchant sent men out into the country to purchase small amounts of produce. Moreover, transfer of money from Edo to Osaka and vice versa would call for an exchange between silver and gold. Money-changing was thus a basic occupation among merchants, and was the foundation of many fortunes and famous families. An indication of the profitability of the enterprise is given by the rate of commission in Genroku times, when the changer took ten *bu*, that is, ten *zeni*, for each *ryō* of gold, a rate that might seem low, but being charged on each transaction, amounted to a considerable income.

57 Pawnbroker's—Tamamaki-ya. As porters and a band of monks collecting alms go by in the street, would-be borrowers bring clothes and other objects to pawn. An official has brought a wanted notice, with the portrait of the criminal. At the back, the proprietor or manager sits behind his railing with his thick ledger and his tree of ticket counterfoils. A woman (possibly the boss's wife) smokes a pipe and warms herself at a charcoal brazier. A notice states that pledges will be accepted for a maximum of eight months

As in every other field, money-changers (56) were sharply stratified. In Osaka they existed in three layers. At the bottom were small dealers, who were often retailers of other commodities, such as oil, or *sake*, and dealt mainly with the exchange of copper and small amounts of silver. They were known as '*zeni* shops'. Next above these were the normal run of businesses, operating at the level of inter-city trade, and performing in fact many of the roles that bankers do today, including the issue of documents for the transfer of money, accepting deposits and advancing loans. No interest was given on money in what we would now call a current account, but certificates were issued that could be used for financial transactions. Loans were usually dependent upon the good character of the borrower, and were generally restricted to those who had money on deposit. The weight of silver required to settle accounts in Osaka was much greater than that of gold in Edo, and so the use of letters of credit and the like was a great convenience. The usual sign hanging outside a money exchange was a large wooden representation of a *zeni*.

The top layer was formed of the 'ten men', ten families who from the 1660s exercised the role of superintendents over the other changers, acting as their bankers and at the same time seeing that they conformed to the customs of the profession. These ten families became financial agents to the central authorities, and acquired the right to wear swords.

In Edo merchants carried on business in much the same way, and in the provinces no castle-town was without them. The government exercised some control, in particular the scales and weights that were essential tools of their trade being inspected by an official responsible for weights and measures. The approved pairs of scales were made by two families only, and the weights were manufactured by the same family that controlled the mints that made coins.

Two other essential pieces of equipment for money-changers, and indeed for all those engaged in trade, were the ledger and the *soroban*. In the first were recorded all the transactions that the firm carried out. It was handled only by the owner and manager and contained confidential information about the turnover and earnings vital to the running of the business. A new book was started each New Year.

The *soroban* is an advanced abacus or bead-frame, on which adding and subtracting, not to mention multiplying and dividing and, if necessary, the extraction of square roots, etc., could be performed. It was commonly a frame about 15 by 6 inches, with 13 sets of beads (17 in Edo). Although mental arithmetic was not unknown, the use of the *soroban* rid one of the necessity for memorising or jotting down intermediate stages of calculation, and skilled users acquired great speed and accuracy.

Apart from its chief use in calculation, it could give an erring apprentice a shrewd blow on the head, and might even divert a sword-blow from a burglarious *rōnin*.

In the castle-town of Takayama, deep in the mountains of Hida province, there still exists the house of the exchange merchant for the local lord. It was he who acted as the channel of access for local merchants and craftsmen, organised the sale of rice and other products of the domain, lent the lord money in advance of harvest-time, changed money and acted generally as the lord's

agent. In every transaction a small commission would stay in his
money-boxes, and he was extremely prosperous. The house in fact
dates from 1879, being rebuilt after a fire, but its structure is
entirely traditional, the region at the time being very remote (*58*).
It is really a farmhouse on a very large scale. The entrance from
the street leads right through to a courtyard at the back. To the
left of the entrance is an office where purely business transactions
were conducted. To the right is a large matted area with a hearth,
over which a kettle or cooking-pot was suspended from a vast
hook. This matted area is open to the throughway, and has no
ceiling, the smoke from the fire ascending unimpeded to the roof
—the house is two storeys high—through the heavy beams that
make up the main construction. (Hida produced much timber,
and heavy timberwork was characteristic of the region.) The
living quarters of the family were further to the right, beyond the
hearth, with windows looking down on to it. In the courtyard area
there is a garden with a well, some outhouses, and at the rear a
range of storehouses for goods in transit and for the possessions of

58 Interior of house at Takayama

the household, constructed with two ends in view, against thieves and fire: the walls and roofs are thick and covered deep in plaster, while doors are heavily plated with sheets of iron and have robust bolts and padlocks. Valuable articles and records kept in the house were often stored in tall chests with drawers and compartments secured with iron bands and fitted with castors, so that in the event of a fire they could be rolled out into the street, crashing through the shutters if necessary. The daily business was recorded in thick ledgers by the manager, who sat in the office, with a wooden railing to keep his desk and his account books secure.

While the Takayama house gives an impression of considerable provincial affluence, to appreciate the extent of the enterprises of a merchant-house, the history of the Kōnoike family has some interest. The founder of their merchant fortunes lived in the village of Kōnoike, near Osaka, from 1570 to 1650, and in 1600 started the brewing of *sake*; four years later he began to transport it to Edo for sale there, in view of the expanding demand from the warriors who gathered round the Shogun, sending it at first by road, and then, as demand increased, by sea. By the time of his death he had three *sake*-shops in Osaka, and was lending money to *daimyō*. He had eight sons and two daughters, and in the division of his property, his eighth son, Zen'emon, succeeded to the largest of the Osaka shops and to the principal part of the family business which was to flourish for over 200 years. The dispatch of *sake* in barrels continued for a while to be a major part of this business, but it fell off later partly because of restrictions on *sake*-drinking by the authorities in the 1670s and partly because practice in Edo changed—whereas formerly *sake* had been sold directly to *daimyō* in their Edo residences, it now went to *sake* merchants in the city, with whom Kōnoike had fewer connections. However, the handling in the Osaka rice-market of rice from provincial domains had for some time been part of their enterprise, although they did not sink much capital in the building of their own ships, preferring to charter them from other specialist shipping-lines.

At the end of the seventeenth century the Kōnoike extended their range to take in the Nagasaki trade, and thus had a part in the commerce with the outside world, dealing in such items as drugs and medicaments, raw silk and sugar. In 1669 this trade amounted to 228,000 *monme* of silver. The house had started an exchange business in 1656, partly to help with the transfer of credits from Edo to Osaka in connection with their *sake* sales, and also to deal with their loans to *daimyō* and to other merchants. After the Kōnoike had joined the 'ten men' on the foundation of this organisation in 1662, their connection with *daimyō* grew at the expense of the others, until they had 122 of them on their books. They handled a great deal of rice which *daimyō* sent to Osaka for sale, and continued in the same line until the Meiji Restoration, when they formed a banking-house, the first Western-type company to come into being in Japan.

The profession of money-changer was thus very important and basic among merchant circles in Japan. In the higher reaches, as among the 'ten men' in Osaka, it involved making loans to *daimyō*, loans that were secured by the rice and other products that the *daimyō* had to sell. To demonstrate further how the economic organisation of the country depended upon the merchants, it will be necessary to give a summary description of the processes and paths that rice went through from the farm up to the rice-dealers. In the first place, it must be realised that most *samurai* received more rice than they could consume, and that although their salaries, and the status that these salaries gave, were expressed in terms of rice, most recipients were in fact paid in money. Only the lowest ranks, whose incomes approximated to their consumption, were likely to take their rations in kind; the same might happen with impoverished *daimyō*, but in many cases these would have been forcing their farmers to pay up in money before harvest-time. There was always a quantity of what might be called 'private' rice available in the domains: farmers would sell part of that which was left to them after their taxes were paid, while money-lenders who had advanced cash against future crops would take these over when they matured, and there was also a certain amount of illicit cultivation. This 'private' rice would be bought on site and would

59 Rice-merchants

find its way mainly to Osaka, as would much of the tax-rice from the domains other than those of the Shogun. The method of dealing with this rice varied from place to place. The picture of what happened to that from the Shogun's territories seems fairly clear. His residence and the centre of his government being in Edo, his rice had to go there. The farmer had the responsibility of getting it to the bailiff's office, or other convenient point, after a preliminary collection at the village headman's store. After inspection at the office it was taken to the port by the farmers again, and loaded on vessels for transport to Edo. These ships were hired for this purpose, with one-third of the freight payable on loading, and two-thirds on arrival. They were not allowed to carry other cargo, whereas the shipping of 'private' rice was paid for by allowing the captain to have one-fifth of the capacity of the vessel for his own trading. The tax-rice had to be accompanied by a representative of the farmers of the district from which it came, usually a headman, and he had to get a receipt when it was put into the rice-store. This receipt he had to take back with him to his province to prove that he had seen it safely delivered.

That part of the rice so deposited in the Edo granaries of the central government which was set aside for the salaries of the officials was distributed three times a year, in the second, fifth and tenth months, normally in the proportions of one-quarter, one-quarter and one-half. Sometimes part of the income was paid in money, at a rate which did not necessarily equal the market price of the rice not forthcoming. In the earlier part of the period it may even have been more money than the equivalent quantity of rice would have fetched; certainly in later years it was less. Days were allotted to officials according to their grade, and for officials of the same grade a sort of lottery was held to determine the order in which they would be paid. Originally the official himself had gone to collect his rice, but gradually this duty came to be passed on to brokers, members of the merchant class, who derived from the proprietors of tea-shops near the rice-stores, where the *samurai* used to wait their turn to receive their allotment. These brokers acquired the duties of presenting the warrants and collecting the rice; sometimes they delivered it, but more often they took it over, and gave the *samurai* whose income it was the equivalent in coin. It naturally developed that they started lending the *samurai* on their books money in advance of the allotment dates, so that in the end they were making sizeable profits from the interest on loans and from the commission for their services in both collecting the rice and selling it.

This sort of system existed in some other castle-towns, but a large amount of the tax-rice from the domains was shipped to the granaries of the *daimyō* whose rice it was, in Osaka or Edo. The proceeds of the rice when it was bought by merchants went to pay the expenses of the mansions maintained in Edo to house the family of the *daimyō* and himself when he was on his compulsory visit. The Osaka rice-market was of a complexity which equals that of many commodity markets still surviving in the West, and involved various sorts of brokers and jobbers, dealing in rice not yet harvested or even non-existent. The main business was done in the streets of the Dojima district in the city, the Wall Street of Tokugawa Japan. With the danger of typhoons at a critical point in the growing season of rice, and other effects of sun and rain, great attention was paid to weather conditions, and brokers are often depicted as peering up into the sky to try to assess the prospects. The role of the merchants can be variously interpreted; they were, it is true, acting as non-productive middle-men, but the facilities they offered in spreading out by loans the yield from a harvest that occurred only once a year and in making money available in Edo for crops grown in distant provinces made possible the working of the extremely artificial system which the Tokugawas devised.

One feature of the Osaka exchange was that, even when actual rice was behind a transaction (as it was most of the time, dealings in imaginary and future rice being periodically discouraged by the government), what exchanged hands was a warrant for a quantity of rice in the warehouse where it had been stored on its arrival. The result of all the trading was that some of the rice went off to other districts. Kyoto, for example, depended for its supplies on Osaka. The local demand had also to be met, and this was very heavy, Osaka folk having a reputation as hearty eaters—one proverb says that in Osaka bankruptcies were due to over-eating, in Kyoto they arose from over-dressing. In the turmoil of the rice-markets there would be circulating those who wanted rice to sell in their shops. The prices ruling in the exchange would decide how much they had to pay, and they would receive their chits for the amount purchased, go to the warehouse and collect it, perhaps in heavy ox-carts (generally prohibited to commoners in Japan, but allowed for the transport of rice and other goods in Osaka streets).

Up to now, the grain was usually still in its brown outer skin. Some poorer people consumed it thus, but it was normally the function of the rice-shop to 'hull' it, often by a pounding machine, before sale (59). Some buyers, particularly those who purchased large quantities, employed 'hullers' who brought portable equipment to the house, and set it up in the street outside.

Although Edo was the natural outlet for a hinterland of provinces, and had a fair-sized rice-market of its own, its turnover was greatly exceeded by that of Osaka. This is also true of almost every other product—oil (derived from various seeds), cotton, indigo and so on, not to mention *sake* and soy sauce from the regions near Osaka—so that not only were Osaka merchants dominant, but also Osaka was the centre of a great network of shipping engaged in transporting produce and goods to Osaka, and from there to Edo. Before the Tokugawa period the main routes for trade had been from Osaka west through the Inland Sea (linking the littoral of Honshū with that of north Shikoku and Kyūshū), and east to Edo, with an important port of call at Shimoda. From the north-west coast, shipping had plied to the ports of Tsuruga and Obama, whence goods had to be carried overland to the northern end of Lake Biwa, thence by boat along the lake, and by river to Osaka. There was a route from the north-east to Edo, that did not go round the Bōsō peninsula, but took to inland waterways from Chōshi. The Inland Sea routes had earlier been dangerous because of the activities of pirates operating from the innumerable small harbours in the islands, but with settled conditions, and the active measures taken by Hideyoshi, this hazard ceased to be a threat to shipping.

In the seventeenth century trade with the continent of Asia was brought to an end, and the construction of large vessels capable of making oceanic voyages was no longer permitted. On the other hand, the routes mentioned above, with their transhipments that caused considerable losses through pilfering and spoilage, were abandoned in favour of single, though longer, voyages along the north coast and through the Straits of Shimonoseki, and to Edo round the Bōsō peninsula. This latter route was developed with support from the Shogun, anxious to bring more rice to Edo.

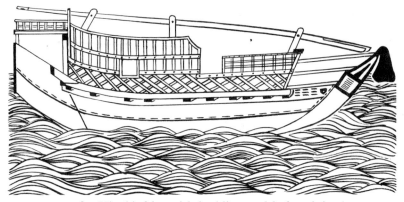

60 Higaki ship, with its 'diamond bulwarks'

From the late eighteenth century it was extended northward to Hokkaidō, which was beginning to provide timber and dried fish.

As for the ships themselves, a description was left by that skilled observer, Kaempfer, as he saw them at the end of the seventeenth century:

> The merchant ships, which venture out to sea, though not very far from the coasts, and serve for the transport of men and goods, from one Island or Province to another, are the largest naval buildings of the Country. . . . They are commonly fourteen fathom long, and four fathom broad, built for sailing as well as rowing; both ends of the keel stand out of the water considerably. The body of the ship is not built roundish, as our European ones, but that part which stands below the surface of the water runs almost in a straight line towards the keel. The stern is broad and flat, with a wide opening in the middle, which reaches down almost to the bottom of the ship, and lays open all the inside to the Eye. This opening was originally contrived for the easier management of the rudder, but since the Emperor [i.e. the Shogun] has taken the resolution to shut up his dominions to all foreigners, orders were issued . . . that no ship should be built without such an opening, and this in order to prevent his subjects from attempting to venture out to the main sea. . . .
>
> The deck is somewhat raised towards the stern. . . . It consists only of deal boards laid loose, without anything to fasten them together. It rises but a little above the surface of the water when the ship has its full lading. It is almost covered with a sort of Cabin, full a man's height, only a small part of it towards the stem being left empty for to lay up the anchor and other tackle. This cabin jets out of the ship about two feet on each side, and there are folding windows round it,

which may be opened or shut, as pleasure or occasion require. In the furthermost part are the cabins or rooms for the passengers, separate from each other by folding screens and doors, with the floors covered by fine neat mats. The furthermost cabin is always reckoned the best, and for this reason assigned to the chief passenger. The roof, or upper deck, is flattish, and made of neat boards curiously joined together. In rainy weather the mast is let down upon the upper deck, and the sail extended over it for sailors, and the people employed in the ship's service, to take shelter under it, and to sleep at night. . . .

The ship has but one sail, made of hemp, and withal very large. She has also but one mast, standing about one fathom behind her middle towards the stern. This mast, which is of the same length with the ship, is wound up by pulleys, and let down again upon deck, when the ship comes to anchor. The anchors are of iron, and the cables twisted of straw, and stronger than one would imagine.

Ships of this burden have commonly 30 or 40 hands apiece to row them if the wind fails. The watermen's benches are towards the stern. They row according to the air of a song, or the tune of some words, which serves at the same time to direct and regulate their work, and encourage one another. They do not row after the European manner, extending their oars straight forwards, and cutting just the surface of the water, but let them fall down into the water almost perpendicularly and then lift them up again. This way of rowing not only answers all the ends of the other, but is done with less trouble, considering either the narrowness of the passage ships sometimes chance to have, when they pass either through straits, or by one another, or that the benches of the rowers are raised considerably above the surface of the water.

Their oars are besides made in a particular manner, calculated for this way of rowing, being not at all straight . . . but somewhat bent, with a moveable joint in the middle, which, yielding to the violent pression of the water, facilitates the taking of them up. . . .

On small ships, as soon as they come to anchor, the rudder is wound up, and put ashore, so that one may pass through the opening of the stern, as through a back door, and walking over the rudder, as over a bridge, get ashore.

The transport of freight was a highly organised business. Much of the trade between the Osaka region and Edo was carried by two shipping-lines. The earlier of these became known as the Higaki (Diamond Bulwark) Line (60), because its ships were fitted with bulwarks of bamboo poles arranged in diamond shape, to prevent the cargo falling overboard when the ship rolled. This line started about 1620, when a merchant from Sakai, an ancient commercial town just south of Osaka, hired some vessels from the havens of the Kii peninsula, in order to start up direct shipping to Edo. It was from this time that goods traffic began to desert the land route. About 1660 the other line, the Taru (Barrel) Line, started the transport of *sake* from brewing-towns like Nishi-no-miya, to Edo. Both these lines were operated in conjunction with warehouses, where goods were received for transport and waited for collecting. In 1772 the Barrel Line had eight of these in Osaka and six in Nishi-no-miya, while in 1773 the Diamond Bulwark had nine. In these years agreements were reached with the central government whereby in return for an annual contribution to funds (known as 'thank-money') they were permitted to come to the following arrangement about carrying cargoes between Osaka and Edo; *sake* was restricted to the Barrel Line; rice, bran, indigo, wheat-noodles, vinegar, soy sauce and wax candles could be carried by either; the Diamond Bulwark ships had the sole right to carry remaining goods. This sort of monopolistic agreement was wide-spread at the time in forming all sorts of trade associations. The 'thank-money' that resulted amounted to a sizeable annual income for the government.

In the 1830s the controls were removed, and in the next decade the two lines were each staging a sort of race in the eleventh month, the Barrels carrying new *sake*, and the Diamond Bulwarks silk, and the first to reach Edo gained a substantial bonus for the captain and gave his ship various privileges for the year. Later the Barrel Line gained the ascendancy and took over almost the whole of the trade.

Apart from these important carriers, there were innumerable coastal vessels working from harbour to harbour, and along rivers where these were navigable, carrying not only goods but also passengers. One of the most important river routes was between Fushimi, a few miles south of Kyoto, to Osaka, and was much used by travellers between these two cities.

Since ships were carrying on only a coasting trade, with rela-tively short runs from port to port, no great attention had to be paid to facilities for crews, apart from a simple awning to keep off the rain, and a fire to cook some rice. Seamen were as weather-wise as they are everywhere in the world, and had their superstitions. Their courage was tested by sudden storms, and they did not hesitate to tackle whales, the meat of which was a delicacy. Local fishing was carried on all along the coastline, and was highly organised near the great towns.

61 Chair-men wait for a fare. They could be rough characters, as is indicated by the tattooing on their backs and shoulders

The spirit of free enterprise, which might euphemistically be said to have inspired the pirates of the Inland Sea in the preceding era, remained with the seamen of the far west, around Nagasaki and southwards to the tip of Kyūshū and northwards to the island of Hirado. Here smuggling was rife. Connections from island to island southward led to the Ryūkyūs and a link with China, and there were clandestine rendezvous with foreign vessels.

In spite of the great development of marine transport between Edo and Osaka, there was increasing traffic on the land highway. As well as being the scene of the *daimyō* processions, it was also an essential means of communication both for warriors and merchants. The carrying of messages of extreme importance was entrusted to officials, who undertook arduous journeys in jolting chairs. The chair-men would utter rhythmical grunts as they ran along with a characteristic stiff-legged gait, the effect of which on the passenger is said to have been most uncomfortable. He tried to counter the motion by half supporting himself on a looped strap fixed to the pole which ran through the top of the chair. The messenger who carried the news to Akō of his master's death is said to have been unable to let go of the strap when he reached his destination, so stiffened was he by the rigours of the forced march. The chair-men had, of course, been relieved at short intervals, at the post-towns stationed along the Tōkaidō (*61*).

For the carriage of letters and documents, and of small packets of money, there was a system of express messengers, travelling on foot. Early in the period the Shogun and various *daimyō* organised their own message service; it was a relay system, with reliefs at seven *ri* (17½ miles) intervals. In 1663 the organisation of these messengers was transferred to merchants, who arranged a thrice-monthly service between Edo and Osaka. These nominally did the journey to Kyoto in ten days, with two more to reach Osaka. There were some slower, cheaper services taking up to 25 days, but there was also a real express delivery in just over three days, involving travelling day and night, and averaging more than 100 miles a day, which was available to officials. Messengers working for the government had priority at ferries, and could pass barriers at all times; very often the messenger was accompanied by an escort bearing a lantern on which the word *goyō* ('official business') was written. The same sort of system came to apply to the other great roads of Japan.

When the shipping was flourishing, it was no longer economical to use the land routes for the transport of goods, and the pack-horses and porters that used them were either covering inland areas where a sea route was not available, or were carrying goods requiring special attention. An extreme example of the latter category was the present sent by the great Kyoto actor of the late seventeenth century, Sakata Tōjūrō, to a colleague in Edo who had played a season in Kyoto—a large jar of water from the River Kamo there, so that he could use it for making the first ceremonial tea of the New Year. Tōjūrō wanted to give his friend something of great sentimental but little monetary value, and to ensure its safe arrival he sent it by road with eight porters to carry it.

A look at the founding of the fortunes of the Mitsui family, who, like the Kōnoike, survived the Restoration to become one of the financial giants of modern Japan, will shed more light on the commercial way of life of the times. Originally the Mitsui family was established in the town of Matsuzaka, near Ise, where they carried on the business of *sake* merchants and pawnbrokers. The originator of their expansion was Takatoshi (1622–94), the youngest son of another Takatoshi; their possession of a family name was due to a *samurai* origin. The father is said to have been lacking in commercial ability, and their success in business was inspired by the mother.

In about 1625 the eldest son, Toshitsugu, had gone to Edo to take advantage of the new developments there and help improve the family fortune. At first he worked for some relations who had a drapery there, but in 1627, at the age of 20, he opened a small shop himself, followed shortly afterwards by another in the same district. He hung over the entrances the indigo-dyed cloth, the *noren*, which keeps out the dust and heat of the streets, and at the same time serves as a symbol of the independence and entity of the business, decorated with the sign of the house (*62*), in this case the three horizontal strokes for *mitsu* ('three'), and the diamond representing the four edge-boards of the well (*i*), which together make the name Mitsui. Commercial houses very often had a 'shop name', ending with -*ya* ('house'); Mitsui called his 'Echigo-ya', as his family business had been. He also established a shop in Kyoto, which was eventually to become his main branch.

Meanwhile, Takatoshi was growing up, and in 1635 his mother gave him ten *ryō* worth of cotton to start him off and he went to Edo to work as an assistant in one of his brother's shops. He had a flair for the work, and the takings at the shop started to improve. In ten years he increased the capital resources of this store from just under 100 *kanme* of silver (1,670 *ryō* of gold) to 1,500 *kanme*. He was also operating on his own account; in 1649 he invested 800 *ryō* in one of the other Edo branches while the ten *ryō* of his own original capital had swollen to ten *kanme* of silver, and he was planning to set up on his own.

His brother, however, heard of this, and was afraid that, if Takatoshi's skill was used in rivalry to his own business, he himself might suffer. So he persuaded his mother, widowed since 1633, to recall Takatoshi to Matsuzaka to take over the family business, and the authority of the older generation being what it was, Takatoshi was unable to disobey, in spite of the fact that he was now 27 years old. On his return he got married, to the daughter of another

62 The Mitsui house-sign is to be seen at top centre of this board, with a large inscription *Gofukumono* 'Drapery' below it. Top left is *kakene nashi* 'no fancy prices'; top right is *gengin* 'cash sales'; bottom left is *Echigoya*, and bottom right, *Mitsui*, written in normal characters

prosperous Matsuzaka merchant; she bore him ten sons and five daughters.

He was now planning for his sons rather than himself. His brother, Toshitsugu, was still in Kyoto, but would be the heir to the family property, so Takatoshi set about making an independent fortune; as a first step he built his own residence in 1652, and set up business as a money-changer. As with the Kōnoike, the profitable side of the business was the loaning of money, but, being in a country district, in addition to the *daimyō* and fellow merchants who borrowed money, they also served farmers who needed cash to meet demands for early payment of taxes, or for deficiencies in rice available for tax, and also sometimes for carrying out improvements. Since loans to *daimyō* and farmers were secured by rice, it was only natural that the handling of rice was added to his enterprises. Loans to merchants do not seem to have played a large part in his business, but he amassed a large amount of capital from his other activities.

In 1667 he sent his eldest son, Takahira, then 14, to Toshitsugu's shop in Edo, where he had been before him, to learn the trade, and in 1668 and 1672, his next two sons followed. In 1670 Takahira changed his name to Hachiroemon. He already had a reputation for efficiency, and by 1672 he was trying to persuade his father to open a shop for him. The decision was made easier by the sudden death of Toshitsugu in the following year: the grandmother, now 83, but not too old to be consulted, agreed to the plan, and Hachiroemon opened his retail shop in Edo. His father went to Kyoto, and started a buying depot for clothing to be sent to Edo. They called the business Echigoya Hachiroemon, and began with a capital of 100 *kanme* of silver. The Edo shop employed five or six senior assistants, two apprentices and one under-man; in Kyoto there were four senior men, and the same number of juniors.

The drapers' shops of Edo at this time were all in the same street and numbered 20 or 30. Their size was reckoned by the width of their frontage. The largest reached some 120 feet, but Hachiroemon's was a mere rented property of nine feet wide, although he shortly leased another of the same size further along the street. At first he was unable to get enough stock from Kyoto to Edo to fill his shops, and borrowed some stock from relatives. At the same time, coming into a market with well-established competition, he

63 Mitsui drapery shop in Edo

had to find a way to attract some of this trade. His solution was to introduce a revolution in the method of paying: before this, customers used to pay once a year, at the end of the twelfth month, or possibly in the sixth and twelfth months, and this obviously locked up capital for a considerable period, and kept prices up. Takatoshi substituted the method of cash payment at the moment of sale, and reduced prices by ten to twenty per cent. As can be imagined, this price-cutting did not please his competitors, and in 1683 he moved into a different district to get away from them.

The Kyoto side of the business was also expanded, with a buying department in the Nishijin district, centre of the weaving of high-class silk material, and in the first years of the new century, lengths of silk material imported from China through Nagasaki began to appear in his shops. A little earlier, another shop had been opened in Edo for the sale of cotton material; by about 1720 it had a staff which had risen from 17 to more than 130. This is an indication of the increase of the number of persons who could afford the clothing sold in the Mitsui shops, an increase that arose partly from the growth of the urban population and partly from its increasing opulence. Saikaku includes a description of the Mitsui enterprise. Among innovations which he ascribes to the firm were the specialisation of the sales staff, with each man in charge of a different product, and also the readiness to make up materials into garments at a moment's notice, while the customer waited (63).

A further extension of operations came in 1683, when a money exchange was added to one of the Edo stores. Three years later the family residence was transferred from Matsuzaka to Kyoto, and a money exchange was incorporated in the new building. In 1687 Mitsui became official drapers to the central government, with offices for this purpose in both Edo and Kyoto, but Takatoshi was not at all sure that it was good commercial practice to have this standing, honourable though it might be; he took an early opportunity of excusing himself, and warned his successors against requesting that the distinction be granted again. In 1689 the Edo exchange business became one of the 30 or so 'principal money exchanges' in Edo. These, like the 'ten men' of Osaka, had special supervisory powers over the other persons in the same business, and also acted as money-handlers for the government, attesting to the accuracy of wrapped coin, checking amounts paid in and out, and so on.

Up to now the activities of the Mitsui family had been confined to Matsuzaka, Edo and Kyoto; now they moved in to Osaka, with a drapery and money exchange, and in the same year, 1691, they placed themselves under contract to transfer public money from Osaka to Edo. The basic system was that the Osaka exchange office received the money and agreed to deliver it within 60 days to the Edo authorities. For this they were paid no commission, but they devised a scheme whereby they not only got government protection for their private transactions, but took a small but steady profit as well. As the money came into the Osaka office, they lent it out against promissory notes to other Osaka merchants who had debtors in Edo: the notes were then taken there and presented to the debtors, who redeemed them, thus settling their debts. With the money thus produced, the Mitsui met their own obligations to the government. It seems that throughout these transactions, the money involved was considered as public money, with the result that any failure to pay up would be dealt with accordingly; the Mitsui also used some of their own funds in the transactions, and managed to make them indistinguishable from the government money, so that they too benefited from the protection it had. Apart from the general good of reducing the amount of species that had to be carried to and fro between Edo and Osaka, the Mitsui concern also reaped the private benefit of having the government's money for their own use for two months, being able to charge interest when it was loaned to the Osaka merchants. It was a very safe enterprise, and constituted a major step in Mitsui's development from a trading firm engaged in a fairly restricted field to a nation-wide financial organisation.

In 1694 Takatoshi took to his bed, to which he summoned his four sons who were engaged in the business, and handed over to them jointly the whole of the family's assets, but laying down the proportion of the profits that would be taken by each participant. When he died in 1695, the general lines of policy had been firmly laid down. Risky operations were avoided: for example, there were scarcely any loans to *daimyō*, and no loans for land reclamation were advanced; towards the end of the period, however, this latter policy was abandoned. The Mitsui enterprise is still very powerful indeed, in all sorts of fields, while its drapery side is now the

Mitsukoshi department store chain (*Mitsu* being the first element of the family-name, and *koshi* the Japanese reading of the character used for writing *echi* in Echigo, the original house-name).

There were several other great merchant families, each with a speciality, like the Sumitomo with its mining interests, but the description of Mitsui and Kōnoike will suffice to show the strength of the family association and the authority of its senior members, and the way in which merchants were able to use the warriors and their system as a means to their own family prosperity.

Unlike the farmers, whose code of conduct was laid down by the warriors, the merchants framed their own rules. Some extracts of a typical one can be paraphrased thus:

> Merchants, unlike warriors, receive no salaries, but rely on their daily trading to make money and keep their family going from one generation to the next. They must practise economy in clothes, food, and dwelling-place, and provide for emergencies, such as illness, fire and earthquake.
>
> Since they depend upon their customers for their livelihood, they must treat the smallest transaction as of importance. They must not be discourteous even to maid-servants or children.
>
> The warriors have their code, the farmers their rules of planting and harvesting, the craftsmen their methods of making things, and in the same way the merchants must make up their accounts every day. The mouth is the gateway to misfortune, the tongue the cause of disaster, says the proverb, and one must never use coarse or insulting language to a customer.
>
> The way of life for the merchant is to be faithful to his lord, who has guided him along the correct way, and not to forget duty and gratitude to his parents who have brought him up, and who, by enduring poor food and poor clothing, have made the family prosperous for future generations.

A less moralistic, but none the less representative code is suggested by Saikaku, one of whose characters prescribes as follows for making money:

Early rising	10%
Devotion to the family business	40%
Working after hours	16%
Thrift	20%
Good health	14%

The following, he declares, will militate against the beneficent operation of the above combination:

1. Expensive food and women; silk *kimonos* every day.
2. Private carrying-chairs for wives; music or card lessons for marriageable daughters.
3. Drum lessons for sons of the house.
4. Football, miniature archery, incense-appreciation, poetry contests.
5. Renovations to the house, addiction to the tea-ceremony.
6. Cherry-blossom viewing, boat trips, daily baths.
7. Spending nights on the town, gambling parties, playing indoor games.
8. Lessons, for townsmen, in sword-drawing and duelling.
9. Temple visits, and preoccupation with the next world.
10. Becoming involved in the troubles of others, and standing surety.
11. Litigation over reclaimed land, and participation in mining projects.
12. *Sake* with the evening meal, excessive pipe-smoking, unnecessary trips to Kyoto.
13. Sponsoring charity wrestling; excessive contributions to temples.
14. Carving small articles during working hours; collecting gold sword-fittings.
15. Familiarity with actors and pleasure districts.
16. Borrowing money at more than eight per cent per month.

All these are more deadly than cantharides or arsenic.

In other words, work hard and do not waste time or money on irrelevant pursuits.

6

Courtiers, Priests, Doctors and Intellectuals

The Emperors, descendants of the sun goddess, had had only brief bursts of power since the tenth century, but the Imperial line had never disappeared. Their palace was in Kyoto, where, with a grant of lands from the government, they lived a quiet life of ceremony and literary pursuits. The courtiers who had their homes there still filled the ancient ranks and offices, and still wore court dress, which indicated distinctions of status by differences of detail. At the Shogun's behest, ranks and offices in the Imperial court were conferred on warriors of the upper grades, and on occasions of high ceremony they, too, wore Imperial court dress. The Emperor continued to perform certain centuries-old ceremonies, such as those connected with the planting of rice and its harvesting, but the main reason for his survival was sheer conservatism, coupled with the maintenance by the Shogun of the fiction that his power derived from his appointment as Commander-in-Chief by the Emperor. Travellers to Japan at the time were scarcely aware of the existence of the Emperor, and Kaempfer in fact called the Shogun by that title, referring to a sort of Pope living in Kyoto. However, the Emperors had some consolation in that they did not expect to die in harness. They took an early opportunity of abdicating and living in quiet retirement, watched, of course, as was the incumbent, by officers appointed to them by the central authorities. The eldest son was often still quite young when he succeeded his father. Younger sons became priests, and many important Buddhist temples had their chief priesthood reserved for members of the Imperial family. Under the Tokugawa régime, the Emperor's daughters were not at first allowed to marry, but had to enter religion.

Kyoto was very conscious that the Emperor lived in the city.

Whereas merchants in Edo hoped to become appointed to serve the Shogun's household, those in Kyoto exerted themselves to acquire customers from the court. This was probably not a very lucrative connection, but the prestige attached to it was considerable, and attracted a snobbish *clientèle* who were willing

64 Nikkō, Ieyasu's mausoleum

to pay extra for the glamour of being served by the same person who attended to the 'cloud-dwellers', as the courtiers were sometimes called. The people of Kyoto would occasionally see the denizens of the court as they went about their ceremonial business, riding in their ox-drawn carriages or on horseback. When they made more distant journeys, perhaps as emissaries going to Nikkō to pay respects at Ieyasu's ornate mausoleum (*64*), or to the great shrine of Ise, or to Edo for some negotiation, they were granted the services of the post-stations free, and farmers had to turn out, or send deputies, to act as porters and provide labour.

The language of the court was extremely courteous and flowery, and the courtiers themselves were considered as rather soft and decadent, even though they were treated with the greatest deference. Their pursuits included such aesthetic exercises as flower-viewing, capping verses, distinguishing between and appreciating the odours of heated incense woods—all pursuits frowned on by those townsmen who obeyed the merchant code of parsimony— and more energetic but still highly ritualised occupations like ceremonial dancing to the court orchestra, and games such as football and polo, where the object was not to win, but to keep the game going in a graceful way. They were also able to summon entertainers from outside, theatre groups and puppeteers, to help them pass the time that no doubt hung heavily on their hands. They cannot have had much opportunity to commit offences, but the government had available a system of banishment by which they could be punished if necessary.

In the mid nineteenth century, the court became the centre of activity which finally resulted in the overthrow of the Shogun's government, and its replacement by an Emperor restored to a power such as he had not known for nearly 1,000 years; thus the most traditional of Japanese institutions came to preside over a policy which brought to an end the period of traditional Japan.

In so far as the Emperor had a fundamental religious function, it was as descendant of the sun goddess Amaterasu-ōmi-kami, 'the great sky-lighting deity', and as ensurer of fertility by the cultivation of a sacred rice-field in the palace precincts, rather as the Chinese Emperor was responsible for the crops of his vast nation. The religion in the context of which these functions were exercised was the agglomeration of beliefs and practices that made up what came to be known as *shintō*, the 'way of the gods'. Its gods included great deities responsible for the creation of the world and of Japan in particular, ruling sky, earth and the underworld; there were lesser deities, protectors of families and of groups in villages and towns, spirits inhabiting trees and stones, and living in households looking after kitchens and privies, gods presiding over the prosperity of farmers and traders, helping with crafts, or protecting associations of merchants. Although the great gods, when they took part in the events recorded in the myths, acted more or less like men and women, they were not depicted in human shape, and, like the humbler spirits, were an invisible presence in a sacred area, marked by a rice-straw rope round a tree or stone or an enclosure. The *shintō* shrine was essentially such an inhabitation, with a series of gateways; ordinary people went to pray at the outermost gate, with the inner ones being accessible only to privileged persons. The great tombs of ancient Emperors, and the funerary mound of Meiji, are basically the same: common folk had to worship from afar, but members of the Imperial family and the Household Department could penetrate further.

Approach to the sanctuary could be made only after purification: hand-washing, mouth-rinsing, or ritual purification performed by a priest waving paper streamers over the worshipper's head. Priests lived at the larger shrines. In a normal-sized village or subdivision of a town, this would be a part-time occupation, but headquarters of provincial or national cults had a considerable number of full-time functionaries.

In much earlier times there had been a female priesthood,

whose function had been the mediumistic one of establishing contact between the present world and that of the dead. In the film *Rashomon*, the spirit of the murdered man gave his version of the crime that the film depicts through a female priest. By the time of the Tokugawas such of those that still survived had sunk to the level of prostitutes and village wise-women. There were some female inhabitants of shrines that took part in shrine dances, but in general women played only a small role in the priesthood. Priests did, however, marry, and normally son succeeded father in a shrine which, with its accompanying land, was virtually the private property of the incumbent, although control was exercised on both the *shintō* and the Buddhist priesthoods by an official of the government.

The duties of the *shintō* priesthood were to act as intermediaries between the people and the god. They received offerings, recited praises and gave, or organised, dramatic representations of the myths on certain festival days. There was a great deal of administration to be done—from the giving of amulets and protective inscriptions in return for offerings, to the management of estates, and, in a great shrine like Ise or Miyajima, pilgrims to be looked after. Subsidiary to the priesthood were the agents of the great shrines. They have already been mentioned as arranging pilgrimages for farmers, giving them a sort of inclusive tour. They did the same for townsfolk and they also were prepared to allow people to enjoy the benefits of a visit to a famous shrine without actually going there, by selling to them the amulets and inscriptions that they would have received, and also, for a consideration, transmitting to the appropriate god the prayers and requests that the suppliants would have preferred to make themselves had they been able to afford the time and the money.

Generally speaking, *shintō* priests did not have to practise any austerities. Their religion stresses a full life, with complete enjoyment of the pleasures of food and drink and family life. Even though, before the Meiji period, the two religions of *shintō* and Buddhism were theoretically combined, so that *shintō* gods were incorporated into the Buddhist pantheon, nevertheless, with some marginal exceptions, the distinctions between the two religions remained fairly clear, as did that between the two priesthoods. The shrines at Ise, whose god was the Imperial ancestress, and thus the family god of the Emperor, were the only ones to keep

Buddhist priests off their premises, and they even devised a special derogatory language to refer to them, calling them 'shaven-pates'.

The Buddhist priesthood was quite different from that of the *shintō* religion, as it was not fundamentally an intermediary between the masses of believers and the Buddha. The priests themselves were the believers, seeking by their devotions to climb through the grades of creation to achieve Buddhahood for themselves. The various sects, some of which go back to the appearance of the religion in Japan, almost amount to religions in themselves. Before Kyoto had become the capital in 794, the Emperor had had his palace in Nara, and in this city there still remained the great temples of the old sects, whose beliefs were not remotely concerned with the masses, but who spent their time looking after their treasures and indulging in philosophical discussion. Some centuries later there were other foundations, the great complexes of monasteries and temples on Mt Hiei, just east of Kyoto, and on Mt Kōya, south of Osaka. They were not so powerful as they had been before Oda Nobunaga's persecutions, but were still of great importance. The Buddhism they practised was full of symbolic ritual and arcane lore. The Zen sect, with centres round Kyoto and in Kamakura, the centre of administration of an earlier shogunate, had a minimum of ritual, but concentrated on a training in meditation and search for enlightenment: its austere methods, and emphasis upon intuition and authority, endeared it to the warrior class.

These sects all taught that a man might achieve Buddhahood through his own efforts, although others might help him either by their teaching or by suitable prayers when he was dead and in the underworld, so that he could go more quickly on his way to his next incarnation. The next development was the emergence of the various 'Pure Land' sects, which taught that salvation depended upon the efforts of another, of the Buddha called Amida in Japanese (Amithaba in Sanskrit), who would grant everlasting joy to those who recited in faith and sincerity the phrase 'Glory to the Buddha Amida', for they would spend the rest of eternity seated in the lotus blossoms on the pool before Amida's throne in his paradise in the West.

The last sect to appear did so just before the Tokugawa period; it followed the teachings of the priest Nichiren, and developed a nationalistic and intolerant trend, and also suffered from consider-

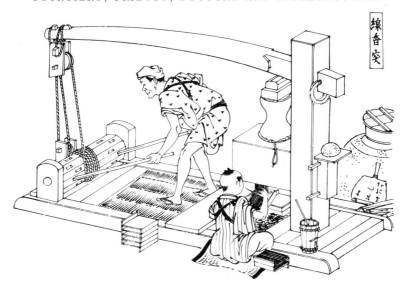

線香突

65 Joss-stick maker. He uses an elaborate capstan for applying pressure to extrude incense, which is cut into lengths by the son of the house, with the boy's hair-cut

able persecution. One effect of the spread of the Pure Land and Nichiren sects was that Buddhism could now become a popular religion instead of an essentially individual matter, or at least, the concern of a community of specialists. The populace could go in large numbers to the services to chant the phrases that they believed would save them in the life to come: and so, although Buddhism had lost a great deal of its political power, which it had formerly exercised in several different ways, it was now in much greater contact with the common people.

Another factor that had an influence was that under the laws against Christianity every inhabitant had to register his religion, and must inscribe himself on the parish roll of a Buddhist temple. The number of temples tended to increase, many new ones being built in villages.

Although marriage was allowed to some of the Pure Land subsects, the greater majority of the priesthood practised celibacy; they had a vegetarian diet, and eschewed *sake* and strong-smelling herbs. The priesthood had its grades, which were reached by a system of training in the great temples, which had an important

66 Two shops for Buddhist supplies. The one on the right, Nakura-ya, seems to specialise in rosaries, while Abura-ya sells rosaries and, on the shelves on the left, funerary tablets. The priests in Abura-ya are wearing their *kesa*

role as seminaries. There was no territorial system in the way that the Christian Church has bishoprics, with a bishop in charge of the priests in his diocese. A priest looked for guidance to the seminary which had trained him, and of which his temple might be a dependency. Under the Tokugawas, at least in the earlier part of their rule, it was the Zen priests who held most of the temples. (*67*). It must not be thought that they spent all their time in meditation and consideration of irresolvable riddles, for they were kept busy with administering their temples and with looking after their flocks; in particular they were called upon to officiate at the death of a parishioner.

The Buddhist priesthood had always been concerned with death. This world was, after all, just a stage in the succession of existences, and the leaving of it was naturally accompanied with Buddhist rites. There was a relatively small proportion of the population which had nothing to do with Buddhism, but were solely followers of the *shintō* religion, and for these there was a *shintō* form of burial, closely resembling that used by the one or two families that exclusively practised Confucianist rites, and involving burial and not cremation. Buddhist rites, however, nearly always meant cremation, and much was made of the symbolism of life ending with a puff of smoke in the great cremation-grounds of the large cities. In country districts Buddhist believers might be interred, although cremation became more and more widespread during the Tokugawa period. Even dead Emperors were given Buddhist rites, as were most of the Shoguns, except the first, Ieyasu, whose remains, transferred from their original resting-place in Shizuoka, were interred at the great and ornate shrine at Nikkō.

When someone died, a priest was called from the temple, and he came and chanted some appropriate passage from the Buddhist scriptures, which were Chinese translations of the originals; the chanting might be punctuated by strokes on a bell (not of the shape that is usual in the West, but more like a bowl), resting on a padded ring to allow it to reverberate, or sometimes strokes on a wooden drum, resembling a gourd. After the reading, the hair of the corpse would be shaved, then the body was washed and clothed in a white cotton shroud, and put into its coffin, which was usually tub-shaped. The corpse would be placed in the coffin in the normal sitting position. The lid was fixed down, and until the following morning there would be a vigil, with lighted candles and burning incense (65), and more elaborate scripture-reading. Then, on the next day, the coffin was taken on a litter to the burial-place or cremation-ground, accompanied by a procession of mourning relatives and priests intoning scriptures. The degree of ceremony naturally depended upon the resources available: a poor farmer would not be able to afford enough for a funeral pyre, and a corner of his land would be set aside for a burial-place.

After cremation the ashes would be collected and placed under a memorial stone in a cemetery attached to a temple or, in Kyoto, in one of the areas that since early times had been devoted to this purpose. A lacquered tablet with the dead person's Buddhist name, given to him after death, written on it was placed in the Buddhist altar that was to be found in most homes, and also possibly in the temple where the family was inscribed.

Special observances requiring scripture-readings and prayers were held at fixed periods after a death. Every seventh day immediately afterwards until the seventh of these (that is, until the forty-ninth day), special prayers were offered for the departed, since it was believed that on these days, and especially on the seventh, thirty-fifth and forty-ninth, decisions were made about the next life that he was to live, so that he was in particular need of help on those days from those he had left behind. If the dead man had been outstandingly virtuous or evil, his future would have been decided without delay, but in most cases, some consideration of his merits were needed, and incense rising from the world could exert a favourable influence. Other commemorations were observed on the anniversary of the death, and here again certain anniversaries were of more importance than the rest; the first, third, seventh, thirteenth, seventeenth and so on until the fiftieth, and after that every 50 years. A devout family would visit the temple on these occasions, and have prayers read, candles lit, and incense burned. The round of these memorial services was a constant occupation of the priest, and a steady source of income.

The family was also obliged to observe a period of mourning, the length of which varied according to the closeness of the relationship between the mourner and the deceased, from 50 days for a parent, 30 for a husband and 20 for a wife, to three for a nephew or niece. This period of mourning was fundamentally a time when a mourner had to cut himself off from the world in order to avoid contaminating others; in particular he had to avoid bringing the defilement of death into the precincts of a *shintō* shrine, and should this be completely unavoidable, he must not go in through a *torii*, the shrine gate. The main entrance to the family's home was also barred; there could be no weddings, no division of property, no drinking of *sake* or eating of meat, no music, and no shaving or hair-cutting. In addition to this, mourning-clothes had to be worn for a longer period, 13 months for a parent being the longest time. This custom applied mainly to members of the court, who wore black, and to warriors, who wore the black *kimono* with the family crest; care had to be taken to keep the head covered, if only with paper, to avoid exposing the sun to defilement.

Buddhist priests would be seen in the streets when going to funerals and to memorial-readings, as well as at the time of the *bon* festival in summer, when the souls of the dead visited the earth, and prayers were appropriate. Novices were also to be seen near the large seminaries, for they would go out with their begging-bowls on their daily excursions for alms, clad in white robes held in place by a cord girdle, a black jacket, a straw hat, and straw sandals or wooden clogs on bare feet. The clothing of established priests varied according to their rank and sect, and indeed according to their means, but the normal attire was the same as the novices, except for the *kesa*, a strip of cloth that hung over the left shoulder and round the waist to the right; the *kesa* was a surviving relic of the robes worn by the priests who first brought Buddhism to China. Their heads were shaven—the act of becoming a Buddhist religious was symbolised by the ritual head-shaving— and they carried a rosary the beads of which could be 'counted' as prayers, or which could be rubbed between the hands, with the beads rattling against each other, to exorcise spirits and lay ghosts (*66*).

A priest away from his temple might sometimes be visiting the home of one of his parishioners, who had a customary obligation to support a temple both financially and morally and often entertained its priests. A priest would be summoned to family consultations, and *daimyō* households would carry a complement of them, not only to look after Buddhist observances but also to act as

67 Manpukuji, a Zen temple built during the Tokugawa period. It shows much Chinese influence, noticeable in this photograph in the pattern of the railing, which incorporates the swastika, a Buddhist emblem

scribes, calligraphers and tea-ceremony experts; priests sometimes delivered sermons, and they were often the only persons available with some training in public speaking. Apart from these respectable pursuits, some priests were not averse to enjoying themselves outside their temples, and the audiences at theatres always seem to include some of them. Many entered into homosexual relationships with temple acolytes, and the boy prostitutes that flourished at the time counted them among their reliable clients. At the same time, the priest who kept a female companion in some hidden room in his temple was a constantly recurring theme in popular literature.

The professional priest in his temple carrying out religious ceremonial for himself and his parishioners had been trained since boyhood. There were also many who entered religion as a means of retreat from the world. These were most often older people, heads of families and their wives, even high-ranking warriors, who wished to give up administration or business and to live a quiet life of retirement or perhaps to become poets and artists. Women might become nuns and live in cells in monasteries. There were also other nuns, or at least feigned ones, who roamed the highways, ostensibly singing Buddhist hymns, but willing to replace them by songs of less elevated content, as well as performing other services. These formed part of a multitude of people on the periphery of Buddhism whose activities overlapped those of street-performers and beggars. They would dance, work themselves into a frenzy of chest-beating or bell-ringing, and even deliver sermons at street corners; at a time when some forms of madness were considered an amusing sight, people afflicted with them would be asked to give a performance for the benefit of spectators. These semi-beggars, who entertained with their antics, merged into the outcast population. Buddhist priests themselves were outside the class system, and in the scale of punishment they were in a category by themselves, being treated much like warriors (without, of course, the right of self-killing), but with appropriate penalties, such as banishment from their temples or confinement to them.

In addition to the priesthoods, there were the *onmyōshi*, who were skilled in the Chinese science of *ying* and *yang*, the negative and positive principles in life. Their concern was with the calendar and the stars, with the compass directions and with physiognomy, and they gave advice about myriad human activities. The date of a marriage was chosen with due regard to the horoscopes of the participants; the date when building a house should commence, the direction in which it should face, the disposition of its rooms, all depended upon their instructions. The choice of the site of Kyoto in the eighth century was decided upon by such considerations, including the protection afforded against demons by the mountains which enclose it on all sides except the south—with the unfortunate result that Kyoto is cold in winter and hot in summer. The practitioners of this lore numbered several tens of thousands in the Tokugawa period, and wielded considerable power. Some Buddhist and *shintō* priests were also skilful astrologers, so that the profession of *onmyōshi* was not always separate from the two priesthoods.

Another group of professional people who were also outside the class system were the doctors. They were allowed the use of long swords, and also had family names. They commonly wore their hair cropped short, but with no shaven area, and so were easily distinguished by their appearance. They transmitted their learning to their sons, whom they also sent to work under great masters in Kyoto and other towns. Their skill was largely based on Chinese medicine, which made great use of herbal remedies. These they prepared for themselves, growing the plants in gardens attached to their homes. The medicines that they used against internal ailments were often effective, and many are still in use; they were also skilled in the treatment of sword wounds, but the knowledge of surgery was not very advanced, although contact with the medical officers of the Dutch factory in Nagasaki brought about a gradual improvement in the knowledge of anatomy, and by the nineteenth century the best doctors were using an advanced combination of Eastern and Western techniques. In fact, in some fields, Japanese medicine went ahead of the West, and the discovery in Japan of a method of general anaesthesia predated that in America.

Medicine was commonly taken in the form of powders, and each person had a formula worked out that suited his personality. Almost everyone carried with him a supply of his particular remedies, and it was a kindness on the part of those passing by to administer to any unfortunate stranger who had collapsed from illness or wounds some of these, which would be found in a box carried on his girdle.

There were some forms of treatment practised by specialists. Very often met with in the evening were the blind masseurs *(68)*, going about their business with their staves, and playing their flutes for recognition. The art of the massage was highly developed, and treatment varied from a quick tapping and kneading of the shoulders to relieve fatigue and strain—any dutiful wife would do it for her husband or mother-in-law—to a full-scale working-over with much pummelling and stretching. Aches and pains and even more specific illnesses could also be treated with the moxa; for this a pinch of vegetable powder was placed on one or more specific points on the body and set alight. It was thought to be particularly effective for muscular trouble. Other practitioners used fine silver needles driven deep into very carefully chosen places in the body (acupuncture). Both these methods of treatment are still widely used, and investigation is being carried on to make a scientific assessment of their efficacity.

Besides priests and doctors there were other learned persons active in Japan. These included Confucianists and also those who studied the literature and history of Japan. The life of the great poet Bashō can well serve as an example of how some Japanese became removed from the class system, especially if they had some literary or intellectual status. It is convenient to refer to him as Bashō, even though it is only the name by which he was known from about 1680 till his death in 1694. His real name was Matsuo Munefusa. Matsuo was the name of his family and, as befitted a person of *samurai* descent, he had the usual array of names used at various times and for various purposes (as well as an unusually large collection of 15 pen-names which he used at different periods of his life). He

68 Blind masseur

was born in 1644 in the small castle-town of Ueno in the province of Iga, and was taken into the castle service to be a companion to one of the lord's sons, whose name was Todo Yoshitada.

Bashō seems to have shared Yoshitada's tutors, of whom one in particular had a great deal of influence upon him. This tutor read the older literature of Japan with his pupils, and taught them to take part in the sort of poetry-writing that was in fashion at the time (the composition of a 17-syllable verse, to be known later as *haiku*, and the adding to it of alternate verses of 14 and 17 syllables, by a group of poets gathered together in a festive way for the purpose). Yoshitada and his companion would also have studied the military arts and the Chinese classics. In 1666 the young master died, and the shock of his death drove Bashō to take up a wandering life. To do this he broke his feudal allegiance and became in theory a fugitive, but he does not seem to have been harassed or pursued. This mode of life lasted until about 1680. For some of this time, at least, he had been living in Edo, under the protection of a fellow disciple of his old poetry-teacher; this man at one time found him what seems a very unlikely job in connection with some water-supply undertaking.

His reputation as a poet was growing all the time and collections of his works were being published. In Japan it had long been a tradition that a literary man could retire from the world into a small hermitage, where his life would be spent in the contemplation of nature, conversation with friends of like mind, and the recording of his thoughts. Bashō now had the chance of living like this, for one of his patrons had an estate at Fukugawa, at the time a country district to the east of Edo, and here he allowed Bashō to live in what had been a watchman's hut in his grounds, and also provided him with food and clothing. Bashō's friends helped him move in (not that this was very difficult, for he did not need more than one or two pieces of furniture), and one of them presented him with a sort of decorative banana tree, a *bashō*, to plant outside his hut.

69 Bashō, on a journey with a companion

They began to call his home the Banana Hermitage, Bashō-an. Hence he became known as the 'sage of the *bashō*', and took it as his name.

In this retreat his life was simple, with the minimum of material things, but great poetical and intellectual activity. There his pupils would gather, coming on foot, or perhaps by boat, and they would write poetry together, discuss their verse, seek to improve their work and to formulate their style. They would augment his patron's rations by the gifts they brought, just as students of the traditional arts even today bring their presents, and disguise their fees in decorative wrappings. Bashō too, in his turn, made the rounds of his own teachers, for Chinese-style poetry, for painting (a mutual effort, this, for his painting-teacher was one of his poetry-pupils), and above all for Zen Buddhism.

During the last ten years of his life, in imitation of Chinese and Japanese poets of the past, he went on a series of journeys round Japan taking the opportunity to visit his family in Iga on more than one occasion (69). For those journeys he dressed as a Buddhist priest, partly perhaps for the practical purpose of passing the barriers without being questioned, and partly because his celibacy, his style of life, his withdrawal from the material encumbrances of the world, and his attachment to Zen Buddhism, all gave him a priestly outlook on life. He tells us in one of his diaries of a series of farewell parties that were given to him as he set off on one of his journeys. His pupils entertained him, and one poet, a former castle-lord who had gone into retirement in order to spend his days in artistic pursuits, graciously sent him a poem; others took him on boating excursions, while some gave him warm socks or money to buy sandals.

He needed to carry only the minimum of luggage, for he relied mainly on the hospitality of former pupils and fellow poets. In return for such hospitality he would criticise poems, take part in composition sessions, and leave poems in visitors' books. As he went on his way, usually on foot but occasionally on horseback—a plodding pack-horse, no swift steed—he would observe nature around him and write poems on what he saw. At the end, when he died, it was on such a journey, in Nagoya. He left, as all poets had to, a farewell poem, *Tabi ni yande yume wa areno o kakemeguru* —'Sick on a journey, my dreams race over the empty moors'—in which his whole life is epitomised.

7

Actors and Outcasts

Courtiers, priests and intellectuals can be seen as benefiting from the increase in freedom which came from being outside the class system, but there were others who might well have preferred to be inside it. These people were deliberately excluded, either because of some personal disqualification, or on account of the trade or profession that they followed. Some were debarred by heredity from being accepted by society; most of these formed the group known as the *eta*. Some were temporarily excluded, or at least had the possibility of release from their outcast status; these were the *hinin*, the 'non-humans'. Some, like actors and inhabitants of the brothel districts, were precluded because they took part in entertainment; such people were supposed to be unacceptable only while pursuing their trade, but in practice for them admittance into respectable society was difficult, since it was to some extent controlled by the activities of marriage-brokers and go-betweens, who would be reluctant to accept as suitable candidates anyone tainted by relationship to an entertainer.

There were, of course, many sorts of actors. Those who entertained the warriors, and even taught them their art, had respectability as part of their reward. This was especially true of performers of the *kōwaka* dances, who performed versions of military tales in the early part of the period, to warrior audiences, and were rewarded by being allowed to wear two swords as if they were warriors themselves. Their status was considerably higher than that of the performers in what had become the aristocratic drama, the *nō* plays. Actors of *nō* were tightly organised into families, either by birth or adoption, and their status within their profession was well defined, depending upon clearly understood precedences. The public of the artisan and merchant classes may

70 Actor's face

not have seen them very often. The Shogun, however, sometimes admitted the townsfolk to performances given in Edo, and there was a certain amount of interchange with *kabuki* actors (performers in the live popular drama) in Osaka. *Kabuki* and *nō* actors had much the same public status.

Although going to the theatre was part of the everyday pleasure of the Japanese living in the towns, the military government was highly suspicious of entertainers of all sorts. Their forebears, the popular entertainers of preceding eras, had been socially unacceptable, being classed as *kawara-mono*, 'river-bank folk', who tended to live along the banks of rivers in the space that was left free from permanent buildings because of the sudden flooding to which rivers in Japan are prone. The connection between actors and river-banks persisted into the seventeenth century, for the first theatres were set up near the River Kamo in Kyoto, in the district where the Fourth Avenue crosses by a bridge, and where the only surviving *kabuki* theatre in Kyoto still stands. The term 'river-bank folk' had originally included members of several handicraft trades as well as that of entertainer, but after the sixteenth century it was virtually restricted to actors and entertainers, who formed the most respectable group of the various kinds of those excluded from polite society.

It was not only the traditional unacceptability that kept actors apart from others; the military rulers mistrusted them more specifically for what they were sure would be their disastrous effect on the morality of their audiences. However, they took the view that the merchants were engaged in such reprehensible pursuits that they were almost incapable of further corruption, so that if the theatre helped keep them from making a nuisance of themselves, it was free to operate. Foot-soldiers, too, had to have some sort of crude entertainment to keep them out of mischief, so that in Kanazawa, for example, the authorities ran a theatre themselves for a while, but did not allow warriors or farmers to go to see the plays. Nevertheless, *samurai* were not above visiting the theatre on the quiet, for on one occasion a special watch was kept on the audience as it left after a performance, and some warriors were apprehended, while others got word of what was happening and either stayed in the theatre until the watch was removed —which was not for some weeks—or escaped disguised as women or servants. For their part, farmers had to be protected—blindfolded might be a better word—from having experience of anything that could make them think that another livelihood might be better than their own, so that visits to towns were not encouraged.

Any sort of disorderly conduct in the theatre was visited with immediate reprisals; the famous Ejima episode has been mentioned (in Chapter 2), one result of which was the permanent closure of one of the Edo theatres, and the sending into exile of at least three of the actors and managers involved. Another, earlier, incident had occurred in a Kyoto theatre in 1656, when an actor had been invited into a side-box by a warrior in the audience and had there been treated to drinks; the jollity had been brought to an end by the warrior drawing his sword on the actor, who fled in alarm. This was all the incident amounted to, and whether the warrior was punished or not we do not know, but all the theatres in Kyoto were closed for some months, and before they were allowed to open again, side-boxes had to be removed and a ban was placed on drinking in the auditorium.

Individual *samurai* became great followers of *kabuki*. For visits to the theatre it was fairly common for them to hide their faces beneath a deep, basket-like hat, but they also saw performances in their houses or in those of their lords. The actors in Edo looked forward to being invited to act on such occasions, and get the special fees that this brought in. We hear of an encounter between the famous actor-manager, Sakata Tōjūrō, and a *samurai*, which indicates the sort of relationship that might occur. Tōjūrō had taken the opportunity of a temporary ban on the theatre in Kyoto to entertain some of the members of his cast to a party in a temple overlooking Lake Biwa. He was recognised by some great lord (whose identity was never revealed), who had him join his party that was drinking and admiring the view, screened from draughts and the gaze of commoners. Tōjūrō was obviously good value as a guest, for the lord insisted on rewarding him with a gift. Tōjūrō was an expert on out-of-the-way presents (see p. 114), and either for this reason or perhaps because he felt that it would be beneath his dignity as the undoubted leader of his profession to accept an ordinary gift, he asked for the pine tree that was growing near by. This caused some embarrassment when it arrived some time later at his home in Kyoto, since it could not be persuaded round a corner in the narrow approach to his house without knocking down a garden wall.

Tōjūrō was more affluent than most of his fellow actors. His house was furnished in elegant and expensive style, and was large enough for him to have rehearsals in it. Being the manager as well as a great actor, he was able to pocket the profits arising from his own popularity and became very rich. Most actors normally worked on a succession of annual contracts, starting from the autumn of each year, the salary for that year being a matter of bargaining between actor and management. In 1741 the Edo actor Ebizō was persuaded to go to Kyoto for a year at a salary equivalent to more than £30,000 in modern British money, but this was extremely high and not repeated. Normally, a quarter of this amount would be the top salary, and the majority of actors would be content with only a fraction of it.

An actor's life was arduous. It is true that he usually had the evenings to himself, for it was exceptional to have performances after dark. However, they started early in the morning and went on all day. Runs were short, depending upon the success of a piece, and, even though rehearsals were sketchy by modern Western standards, there was nearly always some new piece being prepared. No doubt actors of the period had the same ability to 'switch off' as have *kabuki* actors today, for even now programmes are long, and the actor has to conduct his everyday life, entertain his visitors, see to his publicity, and have his meals in intervals of appearing on the stage. The actor had no life apart from the theatre, and this was especially true of the *onnagata*, the player of female roles. Apart from a short time in the early seventeenth century, women had not been allowed to appear on the public

71 Yoshiwara girls (see p. 183)

stage, and the actors who took female parts were expected, if they were to be accepted by the public and the critics (who periodically produced ranking lists of actors) to live as women even outside of the theatre, and to keep any male characteristics, not to mention a wife and family, very much out of the public view.

Entry into the profession might be by following one's father, and making a first appearance in a child's part, or by being adopted by an actor, or by coming up through the arduous profession of a child entertainer. Alternatively, just as a British actor might start his career in the provinces and achieve fame by getting a part in a London West-End production, so some actors in Japan began in the country, perhaps at a centre of pilgrimage like Ise, where the pilgrims' demand for entertainment meant that one or more semi-permanent theatres were kept going, then were fortunate enough to obtain employment in Edo, Kyoto or Osaka, where the great theatres were to be found. Such local talent might be spotted by actors from the great theatres during their own visits to the provinces, which they sometimes made on a circuit taking in many of the pilgrimage centres, such as Ise, Miyajima (otherwise Itsukushima, even now a great tourist centre, with its famous red shrine gate rising from the sea), and Kompira (or Kotohira) in the island of Shikoku, which still has a theatre from the end of the period (now used as a cinema). Theatres at these places were normally set up in open spaces within the precincts of Buddhist temples or *shintō* shrines, both places to some extent being outside the normal jurisdiction of the officials. The actors themselves would be accommodated within the temple or shrine, since many towns had directions from their local lords prohibiting the lodging of actors in quarters that would be available to ordinary travellers. Shrines and temples where there had been theatres still often have votive pictures or stone fence-posts inscribed with the names of their actor-donors, who to some extent viewed these trips as pilgrimages.

Kabuki actors (and this also applies to the chanters, musicians and manipulators of the puppet theatres in the great centres) were only the apex of a pyramid of entertainers of all sorts (*70*). Some of these led a comparatively sheltered life in the restaurants and other places of entertainment. Such were the male jesters whose function it was to do comic dances and sing comic songs and generally make the party go. Their female colleagues lived in their own strictly stratified society, which they entered either of their own accord, when deprived of other livelihood by death of a husband, or by divorce, or for one of the many reasons that might make a girl leave home, or because of their duty to some impoverished peasant of a father, who had received a sum of money in return for their services over a period of years. While one lucky girl might escape when her term was over and return

72 One-man theatre. This ingenious street-performer has made his right side into an elderly townsman or farmer, and his left side into a *rōnin*, or other energetic character. He could thus play a one-man drama

home to make a decent marriage, the father of another might be forced to take more money and condemn his daughter to a further period; there was always the hope that some rich client would pay off the money that had been advanced and take such a woman into his household, possibly as a wife (71).

There were also a great number of wandering entertainers who had no such comfortable abodes (72). The better of these overlapped with the lowest grades of actors. They were the conjurers, the dancers, the singers, the puppet-men, the street-corner men and women of all sorts, whose ranks included the semi-religious bell-

73 Sword-swallower

ringers, chest-beaters and others reminiscent of some of the holy men of India (73). They collected alms but were barely distinguishable from pure beggars, who also existed, and with whom we come to the *hinin*, the 'non-humans' mentioned at the beginning of this chapter.

The *hinin* included not only more or less permanent and hereditary 'non-humans', like beggars, but also temporary ones, who might hope for a return to the status of 'good folk', or whose children might do so, such as former criminals, persons in exile, and survivors of suicide pacts. Desperate couples often tried to die together, in order, they believed, to be able to spend the rest of eternity in a Buddhistic paradise; the authorities were particularly severe on them, and those who carried it through as well as the unsuccessful who survived were treated as criminals, those who died having their corpses exposed as if they had been executed. Double suicides had become very fashionable at the end of the seventeenth century, when the great writer of puppet-plays, Chikamatsu Monzaemon, had written a series of highly successful dramas usually involving some merchant who became enamoured of a courtesan, and ending with their suicide together. Families thus suffered for the sins of the fathers in a very concrete way, but a number of other *hinin* had been reduced to this status because economic or other circumstances had forced them to take up work that only 'non-humans' would do.

The life of the beggars cannot have been much different from what it has been the world over. They lived in hovels and shacks and scraped the best living they could. Such of the temporary 'non-humans' whose families might still have maintained relations with them would perhaps receive some help from them, but the authorities would not encourage this. However, certain employment was available to them; they could work with the law-enforcement officers as jailers in the prisons, as executioners and torturers in the numerous forms of physical punishment available to magistrates; they were also corpse-handlers concerned with the exposure of the bodies of criminals and with the provision of corpses for the testing on them of new swords, and they were the clearers-up after calamities—floods, typhoons, earthquakes and fires—which might result in bodies of victims with no relatives to dispose of them.

All this reflects the reluctance of the ordinary person to deal with dead bodies, a reluctance that seems natural enough, but was enhanced in Japan by the preoccupation on the one hand with the avoiding of uncleanliness characteristic of the *shintō* religion, and on the other by the Buddhistic prohibition on the taking of life. The work performed by the 'non-humans' did not endear them to the merchants and other 'good folk', and tales are recorded against them—how, for example, some would blackmail the pretty daughter of a shopkeeper who might see them as they went by escorting a prisoner, saying to her: 'This man is on his way to death, and craves as a last favour a cup of *sake* from your hand', so that the girl would have to produce a bribe to avoid doing this distasteful service. Actually the 'non-humans' were almost without protectors, and, apart from those employed officially, were marked off from other inhabitants by having their hair cropped short all over the head, instead of gathered up into a queue. A warrior in a nasty mood, or perhaps having a new sword to try out, could cut them down without compunction or fear of reprisal.

In a regulated society, however, no person can be left un-organised, and this was true even of the lowest rank of society formed by the 'non-humans'. In Edo they were registered, according to the district in which they lived, with a leader. The most important was Kuruma Zen'ichi, a name which went by heredity with the leadership. Legend had it that the first Zen'ichi was of an important warrior family, and had tried to kill the Shogun Hidetada (1605–23) in revenge for his brother's death; the attempt failed, and Zen'ichi's life was spared on condition that he became the head of the 'non-humans'.

The *hinin* might in certain cases be restored to humanity, as a reward for duties well performed, going through a form of ritual cleansing to achieve this rehabilitation. The *eta* had no way out of their predicament, being doomed by birth to their outcast status. They, too, were organised, and their head in Edo had the hereditary name of Danzaemon. *Eta* were considered as somewhat superior to *hinin*, and their leader was more important than Zen'ichi. They were marked off by their trade, being concerned with the disposal of animal carcasses, with their skins, and with the leather goods made from them. They lived in certain quarters of towns, or in separate settlements in the country, and could be quite prosperous and live comfortable lives, but it was a crime for them to conceal their origins, or to move from the restricted areas where they resided.

In 1871 a law of the new administration removed all social disabilities due to birth. The 'non-humans' appear to have been absorbed almost immediately into the ordinary world, but the *eta* have taken longer to disappear. Their name is no longer used, except historically, but their descendants are still identified by some members of society and would find it difficult, for example, to marry into a conservative family.

8

Everyday Life in Edo

Life in the country was regulated by the seasons. In the already artificial life of the great cities, the clock and the calendar held sway. The Gregorian calendar, which Japan, along with most of the rest of the civilised world, uses today, was introduced in 1873, just after the Meiji Restoration. Before then the lunar calendar was employed, the year being divided into a mixture of months of 29 and 30 days. Thus, even if they had all been 'great', i.e. 30 days long, there would have been some days missing from the solar year; with 'small' months included, it was even more necessary to make some adjustment, and this was done by the insertion of an extra, or intercalary, month, to keep the year in step with the sun. Such an intercalary was numbered the same as the month preceding it, but with a sign to show that it was additional. Months were, and still are, identified by number (e.g. April is the fourth month), although they did have semi-poetical names as well.

The calculation of the calendar was a matter for experts and was a secret which these professionals jealously preserved. In general the New Year started at a date corresponding to some time in February, which means that it was really at the beginning of spring, and brought with it renewal and rebirth. One effect of the lunar basis for the calendar was that each month started with the dark nights of the new moon, while the middle of the month brought the time for moon-viewing, when it was at the full. The most celebrated moon of the year was that in the eighth month, corresponding to the harvest moon of September: so renowned was this that the mention of the moon in a poem is enough to indicate that its season is this month.

Years were identified by year periods. For example, the Genroku period began in 1688 and continued until 1703, when another period began. The names of the year periods in Tokugawa times had no precise connotation, being generally felicitous in meaning, so that there was a tendency to change them when things were going badly. The system has continued in modern times, but now names are changed at the death of the Emperor.

Buddhism had a concept of a period of seven days, in connection with services for the benefit of the dead, but the week was not a measure of time ordinarily; the month was divided instead into periods of ten days, referred to as upper, middle and lower, and this system continues in use, some shops still closing on the days of the month ending with the same number, e.g. the fourth, fourteenth and twenty-fourth. Days were numbered within the month, as in the Western calendar.

The day was not divided into hours, but into 12 periods, which, at the equinoxes, were equal in length to two hours. The Japanese, unlike the Chinese, used the ancient system by which the time between sunrise and sunset was divided into equal parts, six for the day and six for the night. These divisions thus fluctuated in length throughout the year (not so much, however, as they would in Britain with its greater variation of day-length according to season), and when clocks were brought in by the Portuguese, they had to have a complicated mechanism to compensate for this. At midnight the 'ninth' time started, the numbers decreasing so that the eighth started at 2 a.m. and so on until the end of the fourth at noon, when the series started again from nine. The system may seem complicated to the modern reader, but familiarity made it simple enough to the Japanese of the time.

Over and above the arrangement whereby units of time were designated by numbers, there was another, which came from China, and in which a set of signs was used to give a cycle of 60. Special signs for 12 animals—rat, ox, tiger, hare, dragon, snake, horse, sheep, monkey, bird, dog, boar—are combined with those of the five elements—wood, fire, earth, metal, water—to form this sexagenary system, used very commonly for counting years. It will be seen that a cycle of 60 years will in fact be five cycles of 12 years identified by the animals. From this arises the association of a year with an animal: for example, the first year of Genroku, 1688, was the year 'earth and dragon', and 1700, 12 years later, was 'metal and dragon', so that both 1688 and 1700 were 'dragon' years. It was this sort of calendar lore that was used by the *onmyōshi* (see

p. 132): for example, a girl born during the year of the horse was believed to devour her husband, and thus would have difficulty in getting wed; marriages were often postponed to a date which ensured that the first child would be born outside the unfortunate year, and certainly girl babies born in such a year were much more likely to be victims of infanticide.

The cycles of 12 could also be used to label months (to make up the year) and the divisions of the day (starting from midnight); points 30 degrees apart on the compass-rose were also designated in this way, the rat being north, the hare east, and so on. All this only scratches the surface of the influence that the sexagenary signs exerted and the lore they supported.

The day for shopkeepers started at the sixth time (6 a.m.), when they opened their establishments. This operation was carried out to the clatter of shutters on the street-front being slid back along their channels and pushed into the box-covers that concealed them during the daytime. Whether or not there were bedrooms

74 Room interior, with bedding and other equipment stowed away in cupboards, normally closed with sliding doors. The equipment is typical of the end of the period, about 1850

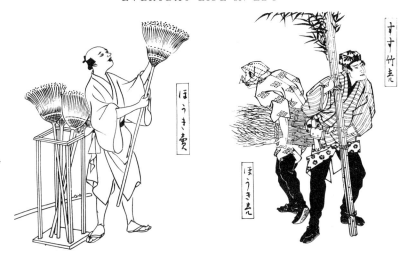

75 Various brooms. The bamboo poles with leaves still on were used in 'spring cleaning', and brooms with triangular heads for floors

separate from the living-rooms depended upon the size of the house. All that was needed for sleeping was a mattress spread on the floor, with a padded quilt to keep the sleeper warm. The pillow was wooden, or porcelain, and was a slightly concave support for the neck. The hair at this time was done up into various elaborate styles, and was fixed into place by a thick sort of grease. It was usual to keep the hair in position for ten days or so, without washing it or doing a major reconfection, and so it was important not to soil the mattress with the grease, or disarrange the hair by sleeping on it. Hence the pillow, to keep the head up. Whether or not people changed into night-clothes depended upon their means. Men and women would don simple cotton *kimono* and tie them with a narrow girdle, but sometimes they would sleep in the clothes they had worn during the day, although a woman would remove the girdle (*obi*) with its heavy and bulky knot worn at the back by merchant's womenfolk. Those with no bedroom, poorer townspeople and employees, spread their mattresses in their place of work, or stretched out on the rush mats or even the plank floors.

On rising the women would roll up the bedding and put it away into the deep cupboards built for the purpose (*74*). On fine days the bedding would be aired in the sun; this airing was done as frequently as possible, because at some seasons of the year the humidity and warmth is such in Japan that unless the greatest care is taken moulds proliferate. The straw mats would be regularly cleaned by being brushed off with brooms (75), and the woodwork of the floors rubbed over with a damp cloth: the effect of this treatment over a period of time was to impart a dull sheen, resembling at first glance the shine given by polishing with wax; in fact no polish and no paint were used in Japan at this time.

Once a year there was a general house-cleaning, called the 'soot-sweeping', when all the mats that covered the floor were taken out into the garden or street and beaten; bamboo poles with pliable twigs were used as brooms to dislodge the dust and soot from the ceilings and fittings. It is typical of the society of the time that this 'spring-cleaning' was not said to be for any aesthetic or hygienic reasons, but for a semi-religious one, so that the New Year could be embarked upon with a home that had been swept clear of the defilement of dirt. The date for this event was fixed; in the first decades of the Tukugawa period it was laid down as the twentieth day of the twelfth month, but when the third Shogun, Iemitsu, died on this day, which thus became unsuitable for such a ritual, it was moved to the thirteenth of the same month. There were local and periodic variations, but the normal practice was to adhere to this date.

The day having begun with the shutters open and the bedding stowed away or out to air, the next concern was the first meal. In most town households there were two meals a day, one in the morning and one in the early evening. Country folk often had a third meal, at midday, but it was not until late in the period that this habit spread to the towns, where it is not even now completely universal.

The style of eating varied from household to household, and depended upon the prosperity of the family, and the status within the family of the eater. The head ate with any important guests, and also sometimes with his eldest son. He was waited on by his wife or daughter-in-law, who were assisted by maid-servants if the family could afford them. The women did not eat with the men-folk, but had their meal separately, either in snatches during their lord and master's repast, and afterwards finishing off any left-overs, or, where there was a young daughter-in-law, she might wait upon her husband's mother. Obviously, in so socially developed a country there would be a great deal of individual variation from household to household even in the same prosperity group.

The normal method of serving was for the whole meal (except the rice) to be brought in on an individual lacquer tray, typically four-legged, about 18 inches square, and standing some nine inches high. This would be placed before the eater. On it were arranged the preliminary items of the meal, those with which etiquette allowed *sake* to be drunk, and which preceded the main nutritional bulk of the rice that concluded the meal. The selection offered reflected more than anything else the occasion, the prosperity of the family, and status within the household. The bottom of the scale was represented by a meal consisting of a soup of *miso*, some vegetables, some rice or rice-substitute, pickles and tea.

Miso is made from soya beans, which are first treated rather like butter-beans, being allowed to soak and then boiled. After this they are broken down to a paste and mixed with rice-yeast, salt and water, and left to ferment and mature for some years: the result is a brownish-red, fibrous liquid that can be diluted in water. It has a characteristic taste and smell. Like all Japanese soups, it was served hot in a lacquer bowl fitted with a lid which could be used inverted as a saucer. *Miso* soup could have vegetables, such as the leaves of plants like parsley and celery, or edible stems or roots, such as those of the lotus, cooked with it, or these could be served separately, boiled and with flavouring, such as bean-paste with aromatic seeds. The soup was consumed partly by drinking from the bowl, and partly by the use of chopsticks, which were used either to pick morsels out of the soup, or to push floating vegetables into the mouth, with the bowl held to the lips. Chopsticks (*hashi*) were often made of untreated wood, and these were thought of as expendable, but others were made, for individual use, of lacquer, or even of ivory or precious metal, and might be kept in a case for security or for travel. A house where the appointments were a little superior would have decorated rests on which to place the chopsticks to avoid dirtying the tray.

Rice, or rice-substitute, such as a mixture of wheat and rice, was cooked in the smallest amount of water possible to ensure that all free liquid was evaporated or absorbed just as cooking was completed. It was preferred that the grains should stick together in a fairly glutinous mass, easily eaten with chopsticks. The rice was brought from the kitchen in a covered container, often of lacquer, but also possibly of wood, from which it was ladled into each person's rice-bowl, usually of china. The method of eating was rather of pushing it into the mouth than of picking it up with chopsticks. It could be eaten completely by itself—certainly no salt or sugar added—or with small sheets of dried seaweed, that were manipulated with the chopsticks to roll some rice in them, the whole being transferred to the mouth, or again with pickled giant radish. This was a root at least one foot long, which could be served in many ways, either raw and chopped and shredded, or, in this case, cut into hunks and steeped in water and rice-bran, in which it turned bright yellow; a superior product was made with cucumbers and *sake* residues.

It was normal to eat at least three piled bowls of rice, and good manners to leave a grain or two in the bowl when passing it for more. Often tea would be drunk from the bowl at the end of the meal to gather up what was left of the rice. This tea was made from the green, unfermented leaf. It was made usually in earthenware pots (*76*), but with little of the ritual of tea-making in England. Tea at mealtimes had nothing to do with tea at the tea-ceremony, where a powdered product was used. With ordinary tea it was quite normal practice to add water again and again to the pot until there was virtually no colour or taste left.

After drinking tea, the meal was over except for a quick use of the toothpick, and a bow and thanks to the provider, be this some deity or the host or the head of the house. When work was to be done, no lingering was encouraged: a quick succession of flicks with chopsticks and it was back to work again.

The range of food that was available for more elaborate meals was considerable. Some things that are eaten nowadays were not included. Meat was a rarity in towns, and beef and horseflesh entirely absent. In fact, in the whole of Japan this was so (for various reasons, partly religious and partly to keep up the number of animals needed for military and agricultural purposes), except that a few *daimyō* families that had formerly been Christian are said to have secretly persisted in beef-eating, while in the Hikone domain, just to the east of Lake Biwa, a local preparation consisting of the tenderest part of the cow, preserved in *miso*, with the hide and hair left on, was used as a fortifier and is said to have been presented to the Shogun and some of his senior staff. Other

76 China shop, showing various types of crockery in common use. The shopkeeper is wearing an apron

permitted meats, such as that of deer, boar and birds, were sold in Edo, sometimes under assumed names, such as 'mountain-whale' and 'medicine', for it was appreciated that the protein-scanty diet of the inhabitants could be supplemented by nourishing stews and similar dishes, to the benefit of the health of their consumers, especially in winter. Even so, meat-eaters were few.

The greatest consumption of animal protein was in the form of fish. Off the coasts near Edo operated fleets of fishing vessels, financed by merchants, which brought in a daily catch, that was sold very fresh for eating on the same day. River-fish also were part of the diet, for angling in the canals and streams around Edo was a common pastime. The fish most often eaten included sea-bream, bonito, trout, salmon, carp and sweetfish (a small river-fish). Although pieces of seabream, for example, could be boiled and used in *miso* soups, and small sweetfish might be grilled, the normal practice was to eat sea-fish uncooked. The raw fish was cut into very fine slices and eaten dipped into soy sauce, or mixed with green and other vegetables, with vinegar poured over all. The tender flesh of young birds, such as the chicks of domestic poultry, could also be eaten in this way. Some fish could be salted, small fry could be sun-dried and eaten whole, and meaty fish like bonito could be dried to a hard wood-like consistency; thin shavings were scraped or planed off the block and used to flavour other dishes or could be eaten by themselves.

It would be possible to list many other things that were available, including crustacea like prawns and lobsters, shellfish of many kinds, preparations from roots and tubers, such as various yams, as well as eggs both of birds and fish, finishing up with exotica like frog-meat and bee-larvae, fish-eyes and fish-skin. It will be more profitable, however, to note the general attitude to eating of the Japanese at the time. The fundamental nutritional requirement was met by the cereal that concluded the meal: it was normally eaten with a certain amount of the husk and germ, so that vitamin deficiencies were not the problem that they were later when highly polished rice brought beri-beri to its eaters. The *miso* soup and vegetables added flavour, some second-class protein, and some vitamins. There was an unconscious appreciation that these three ingredients were necessary to keep life going, for they were not denied to the lowliest employee, food for whom was kept to the minimum consistent with his health and working efficiency. Basic foods were not to be eaten for pleasure, but only to satisfy hunger. Simple meals were eaten quickly, with the least possible time wasted in conversation.

The kitchen in most houses was on the lower level with an earth floor; one could thus go in from the street without removing one's footwear. There was a wooden sink for washing vegetables, with a large water-butt or pot as a water-supply; this

77 Stove-maker. While her husband puts finishing touches to a triple stove, the wife, with baby on back, cuts off lengths of straw to be incorporated in the mortar

78 Porcelain *sake*-jar   79 Lacquer *sake*-jar

was replenished from a well, which was in the garden of a large house, or, in the case of tenements and other smaller dwellings, there would be one common to a neighbourhood, and naturally a centre of gossip and social life for the local wives. The cooking-stove (77) was built up with mortar, with places for the wood fire and holes to take metal boilers—for rice, *miso*, cooking vegetables and heating water. The wooden sink was sometimes used for chopping fish and vegetables, using the excellent knives that were available in a variety of shapes and sizes for various purposes. In all but the smallest kitchens, there would also be a boarded area at the higher level, leading on to the matted area of the house, and on this the cook sat, possibly on thin rush or straw mats, and worked at the preparation of dishes, using an assortment of wooden, china or lacquer containers, basketwork strainers, mortars, pestles and so on.

Although women prepared the meals in the normal private household, professional cooks were nearly always men, trained by a characteristically long apprenticeship. For them the possession of a cook's knife of their own was a symbol of entry into the

80 *Sake*-cups, viewed from above to show the dragon designs

profession; they greatly cherished this knife and considered it as their basic and essential piece of equipment if they set up on their own.

Foods eaten overtly for their beneficent effect on the health were things like rice-gruel, a watery, easily digested concoction for invalids, and occasional game-stews as fortifiers. There was no milk. Generally speaking, all the rest of the dishes were eaten for what might be considered as irrelevant reasons, such as the attractiveness of their appearance, the thirst they induced, or their rarity, either absolute or in the season. It is true that taste was important; with a few exceptions, such as *miso* and pickled vege-tables, Europeans would have found most Japanese foods far less highly flavoured than those to which they were accustomed. The

156

more elaborate and delicate the food, the greater was the ceremony attached to the eating of it. The *samurai* in particular received lessons in etiquette, and some merchants aspired to elegant manners as well. The drinking of *sake* was accompanied in all circles with a certain ritual. When drunk at mealtimes, it was served only during the first part of the meal, and rice was not eaten until the drinking was over. In the home the wife or daughter-in-law would see to the service of the *sake*, which came to the table in elegant china or lacquer receptacles (*78, 79, 80*), more or less bottle-shaped; it was warmed in these containers, and poured into each person's cup—holding about as much as an egg-cup—as he presented it for filling. To do honour to a guest, a host would pass him his own cup and fill it himself, and the guest might then return the compliment. On more festive occasions, perhaps when a group of men were enjoying themselves in some place of entertainment, one of their number might go round the assembly with a full jug and exchange drinks with his companions, and they might persuade their hostesses to drink with them.

Although in most households there were only two main meals, in many homes people would have occasional snacks, and there were many varieties of sweet meats available. *Manjū* were steamed cakes made from sugar and rice-flour, *yōkan* were slabs of bean-jelly sweetened and with various flavourings. There were also many kinds of sweets made from flavoured and coloured wheat-flour and other ingredients,

that were made in many different geo-metrical and represen-tational shapes (such as flowers, leaves, etc.).

81 Itinerant oil-seller measures out (from a square measuring-box) oil into a customer's kettle. The various tubs contain oil for different uses. A strap over his left shoulder holds up his right sleeve. The object in his left hand acts as funnel and strainer

82 Candle-making

These were often eaten just before drinking the rather bitter powdered tea used in the tea-ceremony, and also with the stronger varieties of ordinary green tea.

Activity in almost every house went on until after dark, and there had to be equipment for lighting. Candles were not really common until the middle of the Toku-gawa period; before that time, wax was scarce, because the wax tree which provided the raw material for most candles was not under cultivation and bees-wax was virtually not used. Inferior candles of pine-resin were sometimes to be found, but with the spread of the culture of the wax tree, candles became the most usual form of lighting, superseding the oil-lamp. Their wick was usually of paper. Oil-lamps consisted of a shallow basin of oil with a rush wick floating in it and hanging over the side. Camellia seed oil and other vegetable oils were used (*81*). Candles were sometimes put in candle-sticks and sometimes in lanterns(*82*). Lanterns were made of paper set in a wooden framework, and those which were not meant to be carried about could have either lamps or candles in them. Folding spherical or cylindrical lamps were carried by officials, and bore on them the crest of a warrior family, or a phrase equivalent to 'official business'. Larger versions of these were used at festivals to decorate shrines and temples. Shops would have fixed lanterns outside, with their name or the goods they sold either written in black on white paper, or in silhouette. When processions were held after dark, their way might be lit by flaring torches, and night festivals were sometimes illuminated by bonfires; in the case of *shintō* ceremonial these might be thought of as harbouring the spirit of a deity.

Household equipment was modest and simple. Apart from that for eating and sleeping, it included drawers for storing clothes, either set in free-standing chests, or incorporated into the structure, filling for example the space under the stairs where there was an upper storey. If there was a room for entertaining guests, it would have a supply of square or circular cushions for them to sit on. In winter it would have heating in the form of a large bowl, full of charcoal ash, in which were half-buried live coals. Close at hand would be iron implements like large chopsticks, with which to handle the charcoal. There would also be provided a tray with smoking utensils. Tobacco was smoked in a pipe with a very small bowl, just about big enough to take a modern cigarette; old tobacco-pipes often became cigarette-holders in modern times. The tobacco used was cut very fine, and one bowlful was enough for only one or two puffs before the ash was knocked out into a section of bamboo that was provided as an ash-tray. There was also a receptacle for live coals on the tobacco-tray, and a container for tobacco. The guest used his own pipe, which he carried in a case. When someone called at a house or shop, even if he did not remove his footwear and 'go up', but only sat on the edge of the raised floor, a tobacco-tray would be provided so that he could enjoy a pipe. Tobacco had, of course, been brought in by the

Portuguese, and like King James in England, Ieyasu had tried to discourage its use; in 1612 there were ordinances prohibiting its cultivation, but they were quite ineffective, and smoking was very widespread, among women as well as men.

The charcoal heater was mainly useful as a source of radiant heat for warming the hands and face. For warming the body, the heat was concentrated in a *kotatsu*; this was a charcoal heater with a framework rather like a table placed over it, and then this was covered with a quilt large enough to spread over the legs of those who sat at it, so that hot air found its way up through the clothing, and the hands could be put underneath the quilt to warm them as necessary. It was also possible to sleep at a *kotatsu* (*83*). It

83 Man with *kotatsu* frame

was usual to start up the *kotatsu* on the first day of the boar (i.e. the twelfth) of the tenth month. For applying local heat, live coals could be placed in a special container, and placed in the bosom of one's *kimono*. For the house as a whole the kitchen fire was a more effective temperature-raiser, but its influence did not extend very far into other parts of the house. The chief weapon against the cold was winter clothing, in which silk or cotton floss was used as a lining.

In summer, light clothing, typically of cotton, was worn, and fans, either folding or flat, were used to direct cooling currents of air where they were likely to be most appreciated. Workmen could strip off to the loin-cloth, or at least free the top half of their bodies from their clothing and tuck it into their girdles. Another hazard of summer were the mosquitoes that bred in the innumerable puddles and pools that lay everywhere in the wet Japanese summer. Some protection was afforded by mosquito-nets, which were made of almost transparent netting of cotton, silk or hemp; the largest would cover a whole room, and its shape, and that of those intended to cover a sleeper on his mattress, was of a bottomless rectangular prism, which was suspended from rings on its corners by strings to hooks on ceilings or walls. The air breathed under such a net was naturally more oppressive than that outside it, but when mosquitoes were numerous it was probably a case of the lesser of two evils, especially to someone sensitive to their bites. (In any case, even in the most sultry weather the house was firmly shuttered up at night.) However, there does not appear to have been any

84 Seller of round fans

流し場の内部

85 Men's bath. They show by their expressions how relaxed and pleasant a place this was. One has the key to his locker (or maybe his strong-box) in his hair

malaria in Japan at the time, so that, however annoying mosquitoes may have been, they did not constitute a serious danger to health.

Japan's relative isolation seems to have protected her from some of the worse diseases. There was a certain amount of smallpox and leprosy. There were during the period one or two serious cholera epidemics, but the disease does not seem to have become established in the country. Something very like influenza caused a lot of illness, and the common cold was also rife, while in the hot summers flies and poor storage conditions brought with them a considerable amount of intestinal and stomach trouble.

An important factor in keeping disease in check was the care taken over personal hygiene and the cleanliness of the home. Town-houses did not usually have baths unless they were fairly large, and it was customary to go to public establishments (85). These developed from being places of ill-repute early in the seventeenth century into a public service; in the first decade of the nineteenth century there were 600 establishments in Edo. A bath cost between seven and eight *zeni*. In the early years of the period men and women had tended to bathe together, though precautions were taken to avoid embarrassment. The structure of the building at this time was such that the bath-house proper, where the preliminary washing and communal soak took place, was in almost complete darkness. Moreover, the custom was for men to wear the loin-cloth and women their underskirt even when in the water, or to change into special ones for wearing in the bath. Later in the period it became more usual to have separate facilities for each sex.

Soap was an expensive import item, and bags of rice-bran were used instead in the preliminary wash. No large towel was used for drying; the *tenugui*, a piece of cotton cloth about nine inches by two feet, was used for this, the procedure being to use it wet, rubbing the body with it and then wringing out the water. One did not finish up quite dry after this, but dry enough for the remaining moisture to be taken up by the clothes. The coolness that came from this evaporation was very pleasant in summer, and the Japanese do not seem to have heard of the possible ill-effects of standing about in draughts after a hot bath, about which people in the West are often so concerned. On the other hand, it was considered a good idea to go to bed as soon as possible after a hot bath in winter to conserve the warmth acquired from it.

A complete account of Japanese etiquette would be tedious, but some examples of polite behaviour as it affected the ordinary household must be given. Indoors the correct attitude was that of sitting back on one's heels on the floor. Everyone was trained from childhood to sit in this way, and the joints of the feet and legs had adapted themselves to allow the heels in this position to lie almost flat, sideways on the floor, so that the buttocks fitted comfortably into the cup thus formed by the feet. Men could sit with crossed legs when there was no need for formality, but women were not allowed this liberty. When women were greeting, bidding fare-well, or receiving an order, the hands were placed on the floor and an obeisance was made by lowering the forehead down between the hands, at the same time elegantly keeping the buttocks as low as possible. Men did not go so low. When making greetings in the street, however, one remained standing, and bowed from the hips; only when a considerable superior, like a *daimyō*, went by did people have to get down on the ground to make obeisance when out of doors.

It was thought most impolite to breathe upon people. Thus, when talking to a superior, the hand was held in front of the mouth. The same compunction was present when handling a missive from some elevated personage, or when a *shintō* priest handled some sacred object; on such occasions a piece of paper was put in the mouth to prevent the breath defiling it. It was also impolite to perform greetings while wearing any kind of working equipment. Women, for example, might put a cloth over the head to keep the dust off their hair; they would also wear a band of material going under their arms and behind their neck, in which to tuck the long sleeves of their *kimono* to keep them out of the way of their work. Either of these would have to be removed before speaking to a guest or a superior. Similarly, a man with his towel knotted round his brow to keep the sweat from his eyes, or wearing a pair of the tortoiseshell-framed spectacles that were in use at the time, would take them off before making his bow.

Entrance and exit to and from a room was through a sliding partition. When a servant brought a tray for a meal, she would first kneel down in the corridor before the section of wall that she was to open, place the tray on the floor, and slide open the section; then she would stand up, step inside, go down again on to the floor, bring in the tray, slide the section shut, pick up the tray, stand up, take it to the guest, get down on the floor, bow towards him, and then serve him some *sake*. To a modern Westerner it would seem a tedious business; it involved almost acrobatic skill on the part of the women concerned, but was *de rigueur* in polite households and in almost all inns.

In the best room of the house, the one in which the guests were entertained, there was an alcove, which varied in size, but was often from one-half to a whole mat (i.e. three to six feet) wide, going right up to the ceiling, and at least 18 inches deep; its floor was raised above that of the rest of the room. In it hung a scroll, with a picture or text on it, which would be changed from season to season. The alcove (*toko-no-ma*) was also a suitable place for a decorative pot, or a flower-arrangement, or for displaying a family sword. The most important of the guests would be seated with his back to the *toko-no-ma*, and if the precedence was not immediately obvious, there would be much polite disclaiming of the honour before they finally settled down. The same problem existed when it was a question of who should pass first through a narrow space, although when a man was in no doubt as to his right to precedence, he had no false modesty about asserting it, especially if he was a *samurai* among commoners. In the fairly unusual event of a married couple going somewhere together in public, the wife walked a pace behind her husband and deferred to him in every way.

When a woman became pregnant, the first decision that had to be taken was whether or not the pregnancy should be allowed to go to term. In towns as well as in the country, poverty and the existence of many children in the family might lead the parents to be unwilling to have another mouth to feed. In the country, perhaps because the parents were inclined to wait to see if the baby were a boy, the normal practice was smothering after birth. In towns it was more usual to practice abortion, which was a considerable danger to the mother at a time when the mechanism of infection was not understood. As with many other things that flourished then, abortion was forbidden.

If the pregnancy proceeded unchecked to the fifth month, the custom was to tie a strip of cloth (called the *Iwata-obi*) round the prospective mother's waist. This was done by the midwife who was to look after the birth. There were different superstitions relating to this in various parts of Japan. In some places one of the husband's loin-cloths (they were often made of one strip of material) was recommended, in others she was given it by her parents, in yet others it was possible to hire one from a shrine whose god helped with childbirth. No medical reason is given for this custom, which seems rather to be magical in nature. The months went by with prayers to the appropriate gods and Buddhist powers; care was taken to avoid fatty, spicy and vinegary food. In former times, and still, at this period, in the superior classes, there was a strong feeling that birth in the house brought defilement, so that where possible women were sent to a special building away from the house, erected for the purpose, to have their child, but most town-dwellers had neither the space nor the resources for such a provision, and births took place in the normal sleeping quarters, except that in the case of a first child the mother by tradition returned to her parents' home for the birth. Women were delivered in the squatting position, but in the Tokugawa period a bed with support for the back was devised. The umbilical cord, according to old ritual, was cut with a knife of bamboo, but this had been replaced by one of steel. The midwife's duties were not restricted to attendance at the time of birth; it was she who organised the celebration when, on the seventh day, the relatives and friends came to congratulate the parents on the new arrival. On this occasion presents were brought for the mother and child, who was then given a name.

It was not uncommon to put a child to a foster-mother or wet-nurse, if the mother died or for some reason was unable to feed her baby. The wife of a merchant with responsibilities in her husband's business would be likely to resort to this practice. The

86 *Go* board: pieces were kept in the round lacquer containers, and they in their turn could be stored in the box

child developed loyalties to the foster-mother, and also strong ties with foster-brother or sister inferior only to those with his real brothers and sisters.

In the lower classes at least, mothers fed their children for as long as possible—much longer than in Europe—partly because they believed that they would not conceive again until the last child was weaned, and partly because they kept their babies near to them all the time. The baby was carried around on its mother's back, held there by a broad band that held it under the buttocks and across the back. There it passed the day until bedtime, sleeping and waking as it pleased, being occasionally released for feeding. It would sometimes be transferred to an elder sister, but remained in close physical contact with another human being all the time. At night it shared its mother's bed, and even when a child grew big enough to require a bed of its own it would continue to sleep in the same room as its parents. The constant company of others probably had its effect in later life, when to be alone was felt to be most undesirable.

Most families had a *shintō* shrine where they commonly worshipped, and a god who was their special protector. The child would be qualified by this association to take an active part in certain festivals, and his first presentation to the god was attended with some ceremonial, probably organised by the midwife who had brought him into the world. In circles where the birth hut was still used this first visit marked an end to the period of confinement, and at all levels it tended to occur on the thirty-second day after birth for a boy, and a day later for a girl. For many children it was the occasion when they first wore clothes of the *kimono* shape.

In reckoning age, no account was taken of the actual birthday, but counting was done by calendar months. Thus a new-born baby was one until the end of the twelfth month of its birth-year, after which it was two—so that a child born in the autumn would be counted as two years old a few months later. On the fifteenth of the eleventh month there was a festival called 'Seven—five—three', from the ages of the children who took part in it. Children of both sexes in their third year were dressed in their finery and went to the shrine. It was the day that they moved out of baby-hood, and was accompanied by a change in the way their hair was arranged. On the same day in his fifth year a boy was dressed for the first time in a version of adult clothes. He was made to stand on a *go* board (*86*)—a platform about 18 inches square, raised from the ground, used in the game of *go* (in which the players, one using black counters and the other white counters, tried to surround their opponent's pieces)—facing a lucky direction. Then he was dressed in his first *hakama*, the left leg being put in first. This was followed by a visit to the shrine. A girl went through a similar ceremony in her seventh year, when the *kimono* with narrow bands attached, which were tied round the waist, was replaced by one which required a separate *obi*.

For the children of court aristocrats and superior warriors there was a further ceremony (*genbuku*), to mark the entrance to full adult life. This was more important for boys, for whom it took place at some time between the ages of ten and 15. The significant action was the shaving of the forehead, and the arrangement of the hair to allow the wearing of a court head-dress, which was assumed from this time. For aristocrats' daughters, it was the time from which they blackened their teeth and shaved their eyebrows, as it was the fashion to have them painted in an unnaturally high position on the forehead. Young women in warrior families also had their hair arranged in adult style from the time of this ceremony. Merchant families, too, initiated their sons into adult-hood at the age of 18 or 19; for them it was not a ritual of great importance, but consisted in having the forehead shaved and in donning ceremonial costume for the first time. Women of the lower classes practised teeth-blacking, but only started it either on marriage or on first becoming pregnant.

Throughout the year there were events that the children could look forward to and take part in, even though they were often not restricted to young folk, being part of the life of the whole population. As far as the townsmen were concerned, these mainly derived from ancient practices of the aristocrats, taken up by the warriors, and finally assumed by the merchants. Then, as now, the New Year was a time of much festivity and of several days' holiday. Visits had to be paid to relatives, patrons and all others to whom one owed obligation.

87 Battledores for the New Year Festival. These examples date from the seventeenth century. Later they became more elaborate. There is a theory that striking shuttlecocks was symbolic of swatting mosquitoes, as a charm against their bites

In the *toko-no-ma* rice-cakes were placed, and pine trees were attached to the gate-posts. Each visitor was entertained with rice-cakes, or rare delicacies, and spiced wine. Children played with decorated bats and shuttlecocks (*87*). If there was snow, snowmen were made, but this was not a special New Year activity.

If there was a girl in the house, the doll festival was celebrated on the third day of the third month. This spread down to the townsfolk during the Tokugawa period, and consisted of setting out in the *toko-no-ma* a set of dolls representing the Emperor and the Empress, with numerous retinue and equipment. The display could be very elaborate, with a model palace to house the dolls; or it might consist of a few paper dolls. Plum-blossom was used to decorate the room, and on the day of the festival, female relatives and friends would meet for conversation and a little sweet *sake*. A flourishing trade was done in these dolls in the spring, and by

88 Kite-seller, kneeling to lower his basket to the ground

encouraging periodical changes in design, the traders concerned
sought to increase the demand for them.

Boys had their festival on the fifth of the fifth month. This day
retained great significance in warrior households, where presents
were given, and officials wore special clothing with long *hakama*.
Daimyō residences had halberds, helmets and other military equipment on display before their entrances, together with banners and
a guard of *yoriki* and *dōshin*. Stimulated by manufacturers and
shopkeepers selling model military equipment, the festival spread
to the homes of townsfolk, where the custom arose of setting out
a display of helmet, armour and weapons on a small scale. At
houses where there was a son under eight, a banner was erected,
rather like a wind-sock at an airfield, in the shape of a carp, a fish
credited in Japan with great perseverance in swimming upstream.
Boys celebrated the day by fighting with wooden swords to show
their budding manliness and by slapping the ground with plaited
iris leaves in noisy mock battle.

168

The seventh of the seventh month was the festival of the Weaver-maiden and the Cowherd, represented by two stars, who were supposed on this one day to be able to meet, when he would cross the river in the sky, the Milky Way. On this day bamboo poles with the leaves on, and decorated with coloured paper streamers, cards with poems about the two stars, papier-mâché models of notebooks, brushes and other writing equipment, were set up outside the house. On this day, too, pupils wrote poems at school, and it was in a sense a festival of literacy.

There were many other occasions that a child and his parents could look forward to, such as the day that the god of the local shrine went out in his highly decorated shrine, which was carried by a crowd of young men connected with the shrine. There would be music from drums, gongs and pipes, and great jollity. The *bon* festivals took place in town as well as in the country, and were partly serious occasions, with prayers at the local Buddhist temple, but also had dancing and feasting. Children also had a wide range of toys and games for their day-to-day diversion; they had tops and kites (*88*), as well as dolls, balls, yo-yos and stilts, and they played hide-and-seek, blindman's buff, hop-scotch, hunt-the-slipper and touch; paper-folding (*origami*) encouraged the neat, quick fingers natural to the Japanese as a quiet indoor pastime, while in winter snowballing was very popular.

Japanese children rarely had animals as pets. Dogs, in spite of the special treatment they had under the 'dog' Shogun (see p. 36), were seldom seen in the home, except for some Pekinese dogs, imported by the Dutch. Japanese dogs, typified by the fighting breed from Tosa in Shikoku, were strong animals with close connections to the Eskimo dogs of the North. They were good as watchdogs, but also formed wild packs that roamed the country-side. Cats, on the other hand, were often to be found in homes, performing their world-wide function of vermin-catchers, but never, of course, given a saucer of milk. White cats with one eye yellow and one green were highly prized as lucky mascots for shops, as their eyes symbolised gold and silver. Japan had wild monkeys and some of these were tamed and trained to dance for public exhibition. In the home crickets were caught and put in cages, where their chirping in summer helped to make the Japanese feel cool, like the wind-bells hung on the balconies. Fireflies were also caught in the summer and kept in cages. Ponds were sometimes stocked with carp and goldfish. Generally, animals were cared for only if they performed a useful function, for the attitude to them was an unsentimental one. However, Buddhist law forbade the taking of any life, and to set free caged animals brought recompense in the next world. There were street-sellers who sold caged birds, fish in jars and tortoises to the faithful so that they could be released to the air or into ponds; there was little concern with the fact that they had often been caught and imprisoned especially for this trade.

It has been estimated that, even at the end of the period, only just over two-fifths of the boys in Japan and a tenth of the girls were being educated outside their homes. *Samurai* boys had their fief schools, and in the country districts many villages boasted a school of some sort, sometimes run as a charity or as a co-operative effort by the inhabitants, sometimes as a piece of private enterprise. In towns, school-teaching was looked upon as a way of earning a living by persons of various kinds, including masterless *samurai*, or even some impecunious ones who had a master, the physically disabled, widows, *divorcées* and spinsters, and some families who had teaching as their hereditary occupation.

89 Hanging out the washing. A *kimono* was taken apart to be washed, the material then being starched and stretched out to dry

90 Writing class. Two girl pupils bow respectfully to their teacher. One boy is less well behaved. Each desk has an ink-stone and a copy-book. Paper was expensive, and was used again and again until it was black, only the wetness of the ink making new writing legible. Note the brazier with its pokers, the cat, and the holder with brushes of various sizes

Children learned the family crafts at home; a girl acquired knowledge of cooking, sewing and washing (*89*) from her mother, while a boy learnt from his father and his employees the skills necessary to become a full member of the trade, including the use of the abacus for doing the accounts; or he might be sent off to learn a trade from another craftsman. Schools were not required to do this sort of vocational training, nor were they, in this rigidly stratified society, there to help a child to rise in the world—rather they taught the merits of keeping to one's place. Most instruction was, like that of *samurai* children, in writing, and in copying moral texts (*90*). However, there was also a social side, when the pupils would put on an exhibition of work, and the parents would come and admire, help with and partake of the refreshments, and give the teacher a present. Presents would also be forthcoming at the New Year and at the boys' and girls' festivals, in addition to the regular fees (often left to the discretion of the parents) and extra expenses, such as a charge for charcoal for heating in winter.

It is probable that more daughters of merchant homes went to school than those of other classes. Women played a considerable part in the running of shops and trading concerns, if only to see to customers and clients when their husbands were out on business. Even in concerns that had a paid manager, and clerks and other assistants, the boss's wife often had a great deal of authority. At school these women had learned how to read and write, and were thus able to deal with correspondence and the accounts.

There was also a great deal of reading for pleasure. Many sorts of fiction came out of the publishing houses. Books were virtually all printed from wood-blocks, and most had illustrations (*91*). The simplest were mere picture-books, whose contents filled the same needs as today's comics. There were super-heroes, warriors of more than human capability, and in the same area as science fiction there were ghosts and malevolent foxes and badgers changing into human form. This very popular literature, and also the theatre, nourished a strong superstitious fear of supernatural visitors, partly founded on Buddhistic ideas about the next world. Avenging ghosts were thought to be well within the bounds of possibility, and anxious eyes looked to make sure that a stranger with a haggard expression had indeed feet—ghosts were not provided with feet, and tended to float in the air, or materialise from well-heads or behind screens. Beautiful women met with on lonely paths, especially in the country, were not to be taken at their face value; all too often they were foxes—white foxes being the most cunning—in disguise, only too ready to seduce human beings and lead them into trouble.

Such sensational reading-matter as this was on the lowest level. Fashions in writing varied from time to time, but long tales of romantic devotion and loyalty were hardy perennials, and satirical or salacious accounts of life in the entertainment districts were sure of a wide public. A flourishing trade was done in playbooks (*92*), containing the certified texts of successful dramas, and in critical estimates of actors' abilities. For the more serious-minded, Confucianists and their opponents, the pursuers of pure Japanese studies, produced philosophical treatises. Moreover, almost every activity in the society of the time was covered by some instructional manual. There were, for example, illustrated guide-books, sometimes in the form of picaresque accounts of travels, to the great roads and pilgrim routes. It was a society that was obsessed with moral and useful instruction—lectures on how to lead a good life attracted large and avid audiences —and with observing and recording how its members lived. All these books penetrated far and wide, for not only were they sold in bookshops, but there were also itinerant book-lenders.

A girl's upbringing could be thought of as a preparation for marriage for it taught her how to fit in with the new household when she left home. More narrowly, instruction in her new role as a wife was taught in manuals of sexual technique, aimed at ensuring that she knew how to please her hus-

91 Illustrated bookshop. On the right are advertisements for new books. Behind these, workers are trimming sheets. A *samurai* and a passing porter stop to look at the stock

band. The wife had many potential rivals in the entertainment world, and it was good not only for the peace of the family, but also for its economic welfare, that he should spend his nights at home.

Marriage in the towns did not differ from that in the country districts. Informal relationships developing into recognised marriages were probably less common, although at the least affluent levels they certainly occurred, but financial and business considerations were more powerful motives. A new bride's place in the household was as much dominated by her mother-in-law as in the country but there was a greater potential of freedom in the system whereby a son or apprentice would often be allowed to set up a branch of the main business and take his wife with him. Although the normal town wife had to work hard, life was more civilised than in the country, and many a young country girl must have been overjoyed when a marriage was arranged with some family connection who had gone to the town, even though she had never met her prospective partner. When they went to their new homes, wives took with them a dowry and a trousseau of clothes, bedding and so on. One of the many possibilities of financial ruin is said to have arisen when a family with a marriageable son took to spending too much on lavish training in the social graces, and on extensions and redecorations of the house, in the expectation of attracting a bride with a greater dowry than would otherwise have been hoped for.

It was very easy for a husband to divorce his wife; he did not have to give a reason—although it was often for childlessness—but merely wrote a letter saying he gave her leave to go, and certified that she was free to form any other connection. This letter was in more or less a set form, and filled three and a half lines of writing; these 'three and a half lines' (*mikudari-han*) became the popular word for this divorce document. It did not matter if she were pregnant or not, though in some regions, if she reported the pregnancy within three months of leaving, her former husband took responsibility for the child. He was technically obliged to return her dowry and the equipment she had brought with her, but in many cases she was lucky if she had much to take back, although she could, in any dispute, expect support from her father or the head of her former family.

It was characteristic of the relative status of men and women in Japan that wives had no such right of leaving their husbands. Apart from running away and hoping for the best, there was only one course of action open to her. There were a few temples, of which the Tōkeiji in Kamakura was the most well known, that afforded sanctuary to unfortunate wives. The procedure was to take refuge there, whereupon the temple authorities started negotiations through an intermediary with the husband to persuade him to release her. If they were unsuccessful, the wife had to stay in the temple for three years, and would then be free to leave, with her marriage dissolved by the government official in charge of temples and shrines. If her husband pursued her to the gate of the temple, she had only to throw in one of her sandals to qualify for assistance. In fact, once the temple had taken up the wife's case, the husband most often gave up the struggle and released her. The temple records have nearly all been destroyed, but it seems that in 1866 there were four women living out the period of sanctuary, and 40 whose husbands gave them a divorce. Only wives in the regions near to Kamakura, which included Edo, could make use

92 Illustration from puppet play-book, typically violent

of the temple: generally speaking, women were powerless to leave their husbands.

Most of the description of life in Edo in this chapter has been of life indoors. Outside in the street and public places it was a busy scene. Kaempfer was much impressed when he reached Edo, of which his first impressions were thus recorded:

Just at the entry of the city we passed across the fish-market, where they sold several sorts of submarine plants, shells, cockles, seaqualms and fish, which are all eaten here. We kept to the great middle street, which runs Northward across the whole city, though somewhat irregularly. We passed over several stately bridges, laid over small rivers and muddy ditches, which run on our left towards the castle, as do also several streets, all of which turn off from the great one. Among the bridges, there is one of 42 fathom in length, famous all over Japan, because from it, as from a common centre, are measured the roads and distances of places to all parts of the Empire. It is called *Niponbas*, that is, the bridge of Japan . . . . The throng of people along this chief and middle street which is about 50 paces broad . . . is incredible, and we met, as we rode along, many numerous trains of princes of the Empire and great men at court, and Ladies richly apparelled, carried in chairs and palankins. Among other people we met a company of firemen on foot, being about one hundred in number, walking much in the same military order as ours do in Europe; they were clad in brown leather coats to defend them against the fire, and some carried long pikes, others fire-hooks on their shoulders: their Captain rode in the middle. On both sides of the streets are multitudes of well-furnished shops of merchants and tradesmen, drapers, silk-merchants, druggists, Idol-sellers, book-sellers, glassblowers, apothecaries and others. A black cloth hanging down covers one half of the shop. They stood out a little way into the street, and curious patterns of the things sold therein, lay exposed to people's sight. We took notice, that there was scarce anybody there had curiosity enough to come out of his house, in order to see us go by, as they had done in other places, probably because such a small retinue as ours, had nothing remarkable or uncommon to amuse the inhabitants of so populous a city, the residence of a powerful Monarch, where they have daily opportunities to see others far more pompous and magnificent.

Kaempfer does not mention wheeled transport, which was in fact rarely met with (see p. 25). The streets were thronged with messen-

93 *Sake*-shop, its customers including a rakish *samurai*, and a farmer who has left his load of giant radishes outside. The *sake*-barrels on the left are protected with straw. In the background a tattooed drunk is being moved on

gers carrying letters and money, and porters carrying goods on their backs, or on poles borne by one man or more. People were also out for shopping, on visits to temples or shrines, or to relatives and friends. Many of these folk grew hungry and thirsty, and their needs were provided for by innumerable stalls and shops. Apart from the food that was cooked and prepared at home, there was a great range of dishes available outside, to be

94 Story-teller. He has set up his booth in the street, and has attracted a mixed audience, including, on the left, a shop-boy who should be delivering the goods in the cloth hung over his shoulders. The performer uses a fan and a block of wood, which he bangs on the desk, to punctuate his narrative, usually a bloodthirsty historical anecdote

eaten on the spot, or to be sent for and consumed at home. Bowls of buckwheat-noodles (*soba*), flavoured with vegetables, were in constant demand, and seem to have had much the same recuperative effect as a cup of tea has in England. The usual packed lunch was a ball of cold rice, with a pickled plum in the middle; there were many booths that would sell a cup of tea to wash it down. More tasty were *sushi*, rolls of rice wrapped in dried seaweed, which could include pieces of raw fish, or cooked octopus. Hard-boiled eggs were peeled and eaten as one walked along. To keep out the cold in winter, *oden*—boiled vegetables, roots, and bean-curd in sauce—was a favourite. Steady drinkers could find what they needed in *sake*-shops (*93*), where the consumption of their favourite brew was not accompanied by finicky etiquette. Street-entertainers (*94*) were to be seen at nearly every corner, and from time to time a more enthralling show occurred when rowdy *samurai* drew their swords, although it was then better to keep at a distance.

Violence of this kind had been more common in the seventeenth century than later in the period, when the police had become more efficient. In the 1600s, among the *hatamoto* or 'banner-men' (*samurai* who had direct access to the Shogun), were some young men whose duties were very light but who still had a comfortable income. They formed gangs, one of which, for example, was called the 'White Hilt Mob', who wore white *obi* and white fittings to their swords, which were longer than usual. They adopted eccentricity of dress, wearing a single short *kimono* in winter, and three long ones in the summer; they put lead along the bottom edge of their clothes, to make them swing. When they were short of funds they would not pay their bills; when they had money, they loftily paid in large coins and grew violent if change were offered. A member of another gang is said to have been grappled with from behind to stop him attacking someone, and to have retaliated by stabbing the intervener with a blow that pierced his own body first, thus putting an end both to himself and to the man who had tried to restrain him. At the same time there were gangs of low-class townsmen—porters, labourers and so on—who took to wearing long swords and often came into bloody conflict with the bannermen. These townsmen gangs were also professional organisers of gambling. They too had nearly all been suppressed by the beginning of the eighteenth century.

95 Town riot in 1866

In 1733, 1787 and 1866 (95) disturbances of another sort occurred, when some of the more impoverished inhabitants of Edo attacked rice-shops. The 1787 riots, for example, occurred at a time of famine, when prices were very high, and were not confined to Edo, there being similar risings in Kyoto and Nagasaki at about the same time. The rioters, who numbered some 5,000 in Edo, had for the most part recently come in from the country districts, and were mainly dependent upon occasional earnings. The riots were directed against rice-shops and rich merchant-houses, with breaking in and smashing of fittings and furnishings. The authorities tended to allow

96 Nightwatchman going on his rounds with his clappers

them to work off their ill-will unchecked on such occasions—after all, they were only attacking merchants, who needed to have their pride humbled from time to time; it would have been a different matter if *samurai* had been attacked. In 1787, however, matters reached such a state of confusion that 30 arrests had to be made before things returned to normal.

One of the measures that had been brought in to control the gangs had been the setting up in 1645 of gates to the various areas of Edo. The local inhabitants' organisations had to provide gate-keepers, and at ten o'clock the barriers were closed for the night. This meant that people could move about in their immediate neighbourhood, but could not go more than a few hundred yards away from home. The gates opened again at dawn.

It was not possible to leave these gates unattended because, in the case of fire, they had to be opened. There is a famous story

179

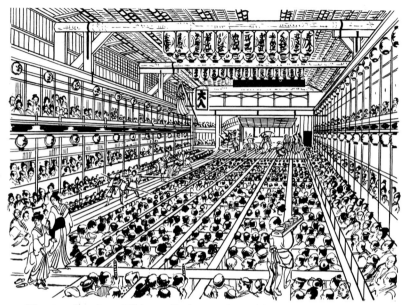

97 Theatre in 1804. This preliminary sketch for a colour print shows theatre in Sakai ward in Edo, on the occasion of the first performance of the season, in the eleventh month. All the features of the contemporary theatre are clearly shown. In the audience are some *samurai* holding their large swords with the hilt uppermost

about a girl called O'Shichi, a greengrocer's daughter, who fell in love with a young priest when her family took refuge in his temple after fire had destroyed their home. After her return, her longing to meet him again led her to start another fire, so that the gates should be opened and he could come to her. Unfortunately, she was arrested, and later burned for arson.

From 1600 to 1866 there were some 20 large fires and three big earthquakes, not to mention fires which damaged the Castle and not the town. The three most serious fires were those of 1657 (in which 108,000 persons died and half the city was laid waste), 1772 (started deliberately by a robber, and destroying more than half of Edo), and 1806 (which burnt out the eastern end, including nearly all the warriors' lodgings). There were also innumerable small fires that were kept under control. The Japanese house, constructed of resinous timber, with paper-covered screens, needed very little to set it alight; if a strong wind were blowing, fire could quickly spread out of control. This is why people with valuables kept them in fireproof storehouses, or in chests fitted with castors to allow them to be pushed easily into the streets through the walls. They were always prepared to snatch up portable objects and leave their homes.

As Kaempfer observed, fire-fighters were well organised (*98*). In 1629 the central government set up the first body of this sort, and soon the problem was being attacked from several directions. Thatched roofs were prohibited, but wooden shingles allowed. Large tubs of water and piles of buckets were provided in the streets. Open spaces were cleared and streets broadened to act as fire-breaks. By the end of the seventeenth century there were squads organised by the *daimyō* and the central government, mainly to protect the Castle and its surrounding ring of *samurai* residences, and by the merchants, for their own property. The central government's men were organised very much like the police. They had leather protective clothing and helmets with hoods. The townsmen engaged builders, especially roofers and tilers, and dressed them in heavy cotton clothing. Hooks were used to pull down burning roofs, and in the 1760s wooden pumps were introduced to project streams of water. Fire-towers were erected throughout the city, and were equipped with bells for the alarm to be sounded, the distance and magnitude of the fire being indicated by the rhythm and violence of the strokes. There is no doubt that many potentially serious fires were extinguished by quick and resolute action.

Townsmen were denied some of the entertainments

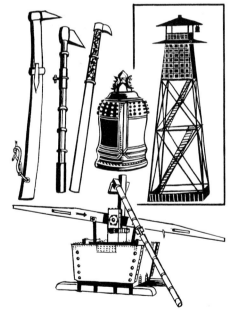

98 Fire-fighting tools and watch-tower

99 Party i

enjoyed by their social superiors, especially during the first half
of the period. Later, class barriers began to break down, as *samurai*
whose income was inadequate began to earn money in trade, and
rich merchants with social aspirations not only took up hobbies
and pursuits formerly considered as outside their sphere, but
also bought adoption into *samurai* families for themselves or their
sons. But in the seventeenth century the townsmen sought their
own entertainment, which became centred upon two closely
connected phenomena, the popular theatre and the brothel
district.

The Tokugawa government had the military mind's approach
to prostitution. It recognised that the lower orders needed sexual

oshiwara

outlets, but was very anxious that uncontrolled licence should not be given freedom to develop. It therefore set up districts in the great cities where brothels were concentrated and where an eye could be kept on them; it also allowed travellers to be entertained in the post-stations on the main roads. The district in Edo was known as Yoshiwara, a name which originally signified 'reed-plain', from the nature of the ground where it had been set up; later one of the characters used in writing the name was changed to another with the same pronunciation so that it came to mean 'lucky plain'. Yoshiwara was not very lucky at first, for between its foundation in 1617 and 1643 it was burnt down no less than four times; partly because of this, and partly because, with the

183

spread of the city, it had become embarrassingly near the centre, it was moved to a site on the eastern outskirts, where it was to remain until its final dissolution after the Pacific War.

The origins and hierarchy of the inmates has been mentioned in Chapter 7. They received a wide training in many arts, such as singing, dancing, music and tea-ceremony, and acquired a taste for fantastic dress, becoming to some degree the leaders of fashion among respectable women. They were described in novels and plays in a very romantic light, as the paragon of all womanly virtues, even of chastity, as in one play where one who has a young lover is persuaded to marry an old *samurai* to free the young man from her influence. When he tries to get his former mistress to continue their old relationship with him, he is summarily rejected.

The customers who went to Yoshiwara sought entertainment at many levels (99). Most went with the intention of sleeping with a girl, her grade depending on the price a man was ready to pay. If they aspired to one of the highest-ranking class, called *tayū*, they might well be unlucky, for she had the right to refuse a customer she did not know or did not like. It required a very expensive courtship indeed for an unattractive man to win her over; a handsome young man was likely to find it much easier. Of course, she could not afford to be too over-particular, otherwise her boss might complain, or even punish her, if necessary by beating.

The ritual of a visit to Yoshiwara started for the real connoisseur even before he arrived. The approved route was by boat up one of the rivers of Edo, to a disembarkation point where horses were available to take clients to their destination. At one time, the true adept wore white clothes and rode a white horse. Arrived at the house of assignation, the guests would call for *sake*, which would be served by men or women; there would be dancing and singing; the guests would be prevailed upon to do their party pieces, there might be games, like blindman's buff, and other revelries that go with intoxication. *Tayū* might be persuaded to join in, and most would pair up for the remainder of the night. There were no doubt some who went only for the revelry, and left in time to get home before the gates shut for the night; most stayed till morning, and went back first light. It has been estimated that in the 1680s the total cost of a night with a *tayū* would be the equivalent of £175 or $420, so that it was a pleasure to be enjoyed only rarely unless one were very wealthy. However, it was possible to get a certain

100 Pilgrimage to Ise

amount of fun in Yoshiwara without spending any money at all. At the front of the houses, bordering on the street, there were rooms with wooden grills; as an advertisement for the delights available within, girls of the lower grades would sit here, and sometimes engage in conversation and banter with the passers-by. It was not advisable, however, to make too much of a habit of being a mere spectator, for this would soon expose a man to abuse from the girls and even violence from their employers.

Yoshiwara was under the control of the town magistrates, who kept a close watch on things. In particular, they had to be informed if anyone showed an inclination to take up permanent residence, in case he was a fugitive from justice.

There was a certain amount of moral condemnation of indulgence by men in the pleasures of the gay district. A wife, however jealous she might feel, was nevertheless expected to maintain a dutiful front; her role was to produce and bring up her husband's children, to look after his home and help with his business. While most husbands doubtless valued the security and comfort that their wives gave them, they also claimed the freedom of having an evening out when they felt so inclined, if only to the extent of taking a drink or two. The main objection to profligacy was economic. When a man wasted his substance he was offending against the merchant code of thrift, and was also depriving his descendants of their due inheritance. No mention seems to be made of the dangers of contracting venereal disease; this may have been restricted to Nagasaki, where foreigners maintained a pool of infection.

The economic censure was often outweighed by the great glamour attached to knowing how to behave in Yoshiwara. Much popular literature is concerned with the comical attempts of country bumpkins to get into this sort of society, and with how ridiculous they made themselves by their boorishness and lack of savoir-faire; but for a real connoisseur to keep his reputation, a dutiful wife might make economies at home and even sell her clothes to provide funds to enable him to continue his activities.

101 Theatre street

A woman's pleasures lay mostly in her domestic duties, and in gossiping with her neighbours at the pump or at the bathhouse. When she had a daughter-in-law to run the home, she might be able to go on Buddhistic excursions, either short local ones or the more extended tours taking in, for example, the 33 Kannon of Kyūshū. She and her husband might go off on a pilgrimage to Ise (100) or one of the other great shrines, though it was equally probable that her husband might go without her, the better to enjoy the incidental pleasures of the inns on the way, where maids were often accommodating, and of the entertainment areas at the shrines. In the great towns of Edo, Kyoto, and Osaka, however, she would be able to go to the theatre (*101*). Particularly since the 1680s, women had formed a large part of the audience, and to a certain extent the early tendencies of the live theatre, with its representation of violence and overt eroticism, had been adapted to a family audience. After an initial popularity in the seventeenth century, when the unsophisticated soldiery and their counterparts among the townsmen had enjoyed blood and thunder plays, the puppet drama had more or less disappeared in Edo. The three live theatres in the city sometimes changed their sites, but were always kept near to each other, for ease of control by the authorities. Theatres closed in the summer, but for the rest of the year programmes changed every month, depending upon the popularity of the pieces; throughout the period new plays were being written, so that the audiences could always see a mixture of old favourites and novelties.

Performances sometimes started as early as four o'clock in the morning, but the first pieces were either ritualistic curtain-raisers or try-outs for inexperienced actors, so that it was six or seven before there was anything worth seeing. Even so, it was often more convenient to spend the previous night in a near-by restaurant, and sometimes it was necessary to do so to get a good place when a popular actor was playing. The performance ended at four or five in the afternoon, and persons who had travelled some distance would sometimes spend another night in the vicinity before returning home.

The seating in the theatre was on mats in square compartments, holding about six people, separated by raised divisions, along which members of the audience made their way (*97*). The sellers of food and drink also reached their customers along these narrow footways. The actors were resigned to receiving no great concentration from their audiences, when the day was so long and distractions so many, and the use of stamping dances and wooden clappers to emphasise moments of high emotion helped to draw attention when it was most necessary. The gangway through the auditorium (the *hanamichi*), along which the more striking entrances and exits were made, also helped in establishing communication.

The invention in 1758 of the revolving stage made performances more spectacular. The light in the theatres was dim, although there were windows in the roof, and so gestures were large and expansive, make-up vivid, and costume exaggerated. Half of the repertory was derived from the puppet-plays, and the formal actions of the puppets had been adapted into the range of live acting. Plays grew more sophisticated as the years went by, but a constant theme was the conflict of loyalty to one's lord, one's parents, one's family (in that order and sometimes conflicting within themselves), and one's human affections. The only sign of social criticism was when some dashing hero of merchant stock was triumphant over a wicked *samurai*. This did not happen often, and most plots reinforced the ideas of social stability that were the official doctrine.

The wood-block prints, for which this period is famous, existed largely as publicity material for the various entertainment districts. Courtesans and actors had their fans, who bought these prints from special shops and used them as decoration about the home (*102*); they were not considered to have any artistic value at the time.

In the open spaces and broad streets established as fire-breaks, semi-permanent booths were set up. There the passers-by would

102 Actor print, typical publicity material for actors of the time

pay to see wonders, such as strange birds and beasts from foreign lands (brought by the enterprising Dutch), monsters, such as mermaids, and people with deformities. Archery-galleries offered prizes for those skilful with the small bows that were used there. Story-tellers practised their art with a repertory that often told of townsmen tricking a stupid *samurai*.

The prize-fights of the West were represented by *sumō*, Japanese wrestling (*103*). This was an ancient sport, which was originally performed at shrines and temples as part of religious festivals. The first bouts to which audiences paid for admission were in aid of the rebuilding funds of the religious centres where they were held. Later the takings went to defray the cost of the presentation and to pay the wrestlers. The basis of the sport is that two men dressed only in elaborate loin-cloths fight in a small ring to see who can throw the other to the ground or force him out of the ring. Bouts were preceded by much ritual, but were short and sharp once the wrestling started. Winners were judged by a referee and received prizes; their overall performance was considered in the promotions and demotions in the ranking lists, positions in which were indicated by a series of ranks. *Sumō* meetings were like theatres in that a tower was raised at the entrance, from which a drum was played

103 *Sumō* wrestlers grapple under the eye of the referee with his metal fan. On the right a former wrestler acts as a superior judge. The ring is bounded by straw-bales

during the fights. This tower indicated that the meeting had official approval. From about 1780 *sumō* meetings lasted for ten fine days; since they were not under cover, rain brought them to a temporary halt. Then, as now, *sumō*-fighters grew very large, and were the recipients of much popular acclaim, counting women as well as men, not to mention *daimyō* and the Shogun himself, among their fans.

A big problem remains about everyday life in Tokugawa Japan. On the one hand, the governments, central and local, were continually issuing edicts to restrict the freedom of the populace, yet, on the other hand, the inhabitants often seemed to do more or less as they liked. Countrymen were not allowed to leave their land, yet they constantly migrated to the towns; in the great towns attempts were made to control dress and almost every other aspect of daily life, but the mere fact that such directives were issued again and again indicates their ineffectiveness. One thing that seems clear is that money talked. Even in the country, where it was relatively scarce, officials could be bribed to overlook, for example, new fields, so that the farmers could keep their crops for themselves. In towns, there were many favours that merchants and craftsmen could make to *samurai*, and the system of gifts which were nearly always given to a superior is difficult to distinguish from a system of bribes. Many officials were no doubt honest, but they were probably overworked and unable to keep uniform control of the large population. It was in the castle-towns that life was the most rigorously controlled, and in Edo, where the control was laxest, for though it was strictly speaking a castle-town it was too large; Osaka was also a large town where life was freer than elsewhere, because there *samurai* were few. And, after all, it was beneath the dignity of a *samurai* to concern himself overmuch with the antics of townsmen as long as they offered no threat to their superiors. So, the motivation of the townsmen lay in their own moral values, and in their human search for pleasures. It was a struggle between a puritanical and obsessive desire to earn money and increase the fortune of the family by thrift, which brought into being a complex mercantile society, and an almost equally strong demand for enjoyment, which brought into being a vast entertainment industry. It is the combination of restraint and abandon which makes the Japanese of the Tokugawa period so fascinating.

NOTES ON FURTHER READING

The passages quoted from Kaempfer's account of Japan at the end of the seventeenth century are from an English translation that appeared shortly after his death and was reprinted with slightly modernised spelling in 1906. It is reliable in everything except what it says about the Japanese language, and should be read by anyone who wishes to acquire a picture of life in Japan at the time.

Sir George Sansom spent much of a long lifetime in a study of Japan, and his last work, a history of the Tokugawa period, gives an authoritative and elegant account. *Japanese Inn* gives a most attractive description of life on the great road from Edo to Osaka, reflecting the changing events of the times. *Takizawa Bakin* is the biography of a novel-writer of the late eighteenth and early nineteenth centuries, and is full of information about life in Edo.

The three translations by eminent modern scholars are also highly recommended, not only for the fascinating contents of the works translated, but also for the vast amount of information that the translators give in their notes and introductions.

Finally, the author is aware that he could have given considerably more space to education and schools. This deficiency can be repaired by reading Professor Dore's work quoted below.

Details of the books mentioned

R. P. Dore, *Education in Tokugawa Japan* (London, Routledge and Kegan Paul, 1965)

Ihara Saikaku (Ivan Morris, ed. and tr.), *The life of an amorous woman* (London, Chapman and Hall, 1963)

Ihara Saikaku (G. W. Sargent, ed. and tr.), *The Japanese family storehouse* (London, Cambridge University Press, 1959)

Engelbert Kaempfer, *The history of Japan*, 3 vols. (Glasgow, James MacLehose and Sons, 1906)

Donald Keene, *Major plays of Chikamatsu* (New York and London, Columbia University Press, 1961)

George Sansom, *A history of Japan, 1615–1867* (London, The Cresset Press, 1964)

Oliver Statler, *Japanese Inn* (New York, Random House, 1961)

Leon M. Zolbrod, *Takizawa Bakin* (New York, Twayne Publishers, Inc., 1967)

Still further reading

Most of the above books have bibliographies, which will suggest yet more titles for reading.

INDEX

The numerals in **bold type** refer to the figure-numerals of the illustrations.